F. Philip Rice
is the author of some twenty books,
including Prentice-Hall's *Getting Rich with Rental Property*.
A professor at the University of Maine, Dr. Rice holds
four degrees, including a doctorate from Columbia University.
He has done extensive study on the stock market,
and in his years of experience using the conservative,
fast-growth investment approach in this book,
he has never lost money and has usually earned fabulous profits.

GETTING RICH
with
LOW-PRICED STOCKS

F. Philip Rice

PRENTICE HALL PRESS • NEW YORK

Published in 1987 by Prentice Hall Press
A Division of Simon & Schuster, Inc.
Gulf + Western Building
Gulf + Western Plaza
New York, NY 10023

Originally published by Prentice-Hall, Inc.

PRENTICE HALL PRESS is a trademark of Simon & Schuster, Inc.

Library of Congress Cataloging-in-Publication Data

RICE, F. PHILIP.
Getting rich with low priced stocks.

Includes index.
1. Stocks—United States—Handbooks, manuals, etc.
I. Title.
HG4921.R48   1984   332.63'22   83-24640
ISBN 0-13-354614-4 (pbk.)

Manufactured in the United States of America

10 9 8 7 6 5

First Prentice Hall Press Edition

INVESTOR'S PRAYER

Oh Lord, give me guidance
in buying those stocks I ought to buy,
in omitting those stocks I ought not to buy,
and the wisdom to know the difference.

CONTENTS

GETTING RICH
with
LOW-PRICED STOCKS

1

WHY LOW-PRICED STOCKS?

Each person has a different idea of what constitutes a low-priced stock. Prices are relative, depending upon your point of view. To a millionaire, $100 may be a low price for a stock. To the poor man, it's a lot of money. For purposes of discussion in this book, a low-priced stock is one selling for $10 or less a share. I realize that this is an arbitrary definition, but it is one that makes sense, as we'll see.

The only real reason for buying a low-priced stock instead of a more expensive one is because you're more likely to make money: not just a little more but a lot more. Of all stocks listed on the exchanges, the low-priced stocks usually out-perform the rest of the market. They don't always, but most of the time they do.

I can prove this to you in a number of ways. Let's take the calendar year 1981. As it turned out, this was a bearish year from most points of view. Over the full year, stocks on the New York Stock Exchange (NYSE) declined 9 percent; those on the American Stock Exchange declined 8 precent; and Over-the-Counter (OTC) stocks declined a scant 3 percent. All three markets hit bottom in September, within three days of one another, and, if a significant rally had not taken place during the last quarter, the year's record would have been quite dismal indeed.

But even during this bearish year, 150 out of a total of 787 stocks on the ASE increased in price by over 30 percent! And out of these 150 stocks, 95 of them, or 63 percent, were selling for $10/share or less at the beginning of 1981. The top 50 performers during 1981 increased in price from 69 to 396 percent: Thirty-five of these 50, or 70 percent, were low-priced stocks at the beginning of 1981. Among the top ten performers, with amazing increases in price from 147 to 396 percent, 8 out of 10 were selling below $8 per share at the beginning of 1981. Is it any wonder that low-priced stocks are so attractive?

What about the worst performers on the ASE during 1981? Out of the 150 worst performers, whose prices declined from 42 to 89 percent, 92 stocks, or 61 percent, were selling above $10 per share. Out of the bottom 50, whose prices declined from 53 to 89 percent, 33 stocks, or 66 percent, were selling for more than $10 per share.

The results are not quite as dramatic with OTC stocks, but the trends are in the same direction. Twenty-six out of 50 (52 percent) of the top 50 performers, with prices increasing from 65 to 386 percent during 1981, were selling for $10 or less per share at the beginning of 1981. Out of the worst 50 performers, with price losses from 56 to 94 percent, 32 stocks (64 percent) were selling for over $10 per share at the beginning of 1981.

Of course, just because a stock is low-priced does not mean it is going to go up, and just because it is medium- or high-priced does not mean it is going down. But from a probability standpoint—as demonstrated by actual stock performance—you have a much greater chance of making big money with low-priced stocks than with high-priced stocks.

The real question is: Why? One answer is because investors would rather buy low-priced stocks than higher-priced ones. It's a question of supply and demand. The more people who want to buy a particular stock, the more the price goes up. The more shares of a stock available to be purchased that people don't want, the more likely the price will go down.

Stock prices are bid up by competition for purchase. They decline by competition for sales.

It's quite obvious that the average investor finds low-priced stocks more attractive than higher-priced ones. Psychologically, it is more desirable to have 100 shares of a $10 stock, than to have 10 shares of a $100 stock. An investor who wants to spend several thousand dollars can pick up 1,000 shares of a very good stock. Wouldn't you rather own 1,000 shares than 100? Most of you would, and so would everyone else, and for a very good reason. If you own 1,000 shares of stock, it has to go up only one point before you earn $1,000 (less commissions). But if you own 100 shares of a stock, it has to up 10 points before you earn $1,000 (less commissions). Most buyers feel that it's more likely that a $5 stock will go up one point than that a $50 stock will go up 10 points. Even though each represents a 20 percent increase, investors will bet on the one point over the 10 points every time.

Look at it this way. A 20 percent rise of the Dow Jones Industrial Average on the NYSE represents an increase from say 1000 to 1200 or 1200 to 1440. This usually takes weeks, or months, whereas a 20 percent rise in a $5 stock can easily happen in a few days or a week. And the potential for maximum growth is much greater on the low-priced stock than a high-priced one. Very few $50 or $100 stocks double or triple in a year, but it is quite common for low-priced stocks to do so. Would you believe that the Dow Jones Industrial Average starting at a high of 1200 would reach 2400 within a year? But if you bought a very good $4 high-growth stock, you might possibly see it reach $8 to $12 before the year's end. It's all a question of percentages. You can expect maximum percentage increases with low-priced stocks if you select them carefully.

Also, buying low-priced stocks is much more financially feasible to the average investor. Only the largest investor or an institutional buyer can purchase 1,000 shares of a stock selling for $50 per share, whereas you don't have to be a wealthy person to purchase 1,000 shares of a $5 stock. Because stocks are sold most efficiently in 100-share lots, the only ones many people can buy at all are the low-priced ones. This puts pressure on these stocks to out-perform the rest of the market.

Years ago, when I was first learning to make my way in the stock market, I started buying stocks in 10-to-20 share lots. They were the only ones I could afford because I rarely invested over $200 at a time. My broker was patient—and cooperative—but even he finally had to tell me that he couldn't continue doing it—it was costing the company money. So I had to switch over to 100-share lots. I had to save my money a long time before I could afford these—even the low-priced ones. As the years have gone by, I have been able to buy more and more shares at a time, so that now I rarely trade less than 1,000 shares at once. But I still buy low-priced ones! And I also save on commissions, but that is another story.

There is still another powerful argument for purchasing low-priced stocks. Many of these are stocks in new, small but growing companies. Some of these have gone through all the preliminary birth pains, have now been firmly established, and are beginning to grow and expand their products and markets. If you're looking for growth stocks, then these are the kinds of companies to invest in. They won't all grow as fast as did IBM at one time, but some are expanding so fast that the prices of their stocks are skyrocketing, and even then, these are not keeping up with earnings growth. All investors hope to get in on the ground floor of high-growth companies, but you are ordinarily not going to find these among the expensive stocks whose long-term growth potentials have already been realized and reflected in their stock prices.

2

APPROACHES
TO
BUYING STOCKS

People buy stocks for a number of different reasons.

INCOME

One reason is to have a steady income. This is the most conservative approach to investing in the market. It is used by those who need income for current expenses or retirement. Those who have this investment goal don't usually get too upset if the price of the stock fluctuates, as long as they get their dividend checks each quarter. These persons seek out solid companies that pay a good yield and whose dividends are rising. This way they are relatively certain of their income increasing in the years ahead. I would only offer one word of caution. Ordinarily, dividends paid out each year should total no more than 40 percent of the company's earnings. If they do, at least over a period of time, the company is not keeping enough profit for expansion or for emergencies. While it's nice to get huge dividends, there is no use killing the goose that's laying the golden egg. The goose needs a little fattening or the eggs stop coming.

TRADING FOR APPRECIATION

This approach seeks to make money as fast as possible—not through dividend earnings, but through buying and selling stocks in large lots for a profit. Traders, as opposed to investors, buy and sell daily, or weekly, taking advantage of day-to-day and week-to-week fluctuations to make a profit. Their profit margins are small, but by trading in huge lots, they are able to make money. This approach is the complete opposite to investing for income through dividends. Trading for appreciation is short-term investing, often in highly volatile issues.

I realize that there are some traders who can make money—millions in fact—but they are the elite few, the highly sophisticated professionals who have spent a lifetime developing their skill at "playing the market." For the average investor to think he or she can make money the same way is sheer nonsense.

HIGHLY SPECULATIVE
GROWTH APPROACHES

There are some investors who trade in the most highly speculative stocks, whose prices may be twenty-five to one hundred times their earnings per share. Their goal is high profits through rapid appreciation. These investors are willing to take considerable risks, with the chance of "striking it rich," by finding stocks in which they can double or triple their money in a relatively short time.

In spite of the fact that this is a speculative approach, those who know what they are doing can reduce their risks considerably and, at the same time, make money fast—their investment goal. However, they don't buy blindly. They obtain as much information as possible. It may be information that is not generally available to the public. They may buy or sell on rumor, sometimes on rumors they create themselves. Theirs is a risk approach, but it is not a blind approach.

Unfortunately, average investors who try this approach usually lose money. They have three basic problems. One, they are greedy. Two, they forget to use their heads. They wouldn't think of buying a house without looking at it first, comparing it with others, and discussing it thoroughly before arriving at a decision. But when it comes to purchasing $500, $5,000, or $10,000 worth of stock, they buy on someone else's recommendation, sight unseen (without really looking into it themselves), on rumor (which is usually unfounded), on a hunch (they have a feeling), or because they like it (but they can't tell you why). They hope for a miracle: to be able to make money on a poor buy. Sometimes it happens, most of the time it doesn't.

The third problem these people have is that they like to gamble. They falsely believe that they have to take a big chance if they're going to buy stocks. "Oh well, I might as well take a chance. After all, life is a gamble." So they approach stock buying the same way. They relegate it to the realm of the unknown—to hope, dreams, and magic. Selecting a stock becomes as uncertain as a spin of the roulette wheel or winning the state lottery. Frankly, if selecting stocks was that much of a gamble none of us would ever buy them.

LONG-TERM INVESTMENTS

Another approach to stock buying is to buy them as long-term investments: for maximum appreciation over a period of years with some income—stock or cash dividends—along the way. This combines the conservative-income approach with the growth approach but without as much speculative risk. It is one of the soundest approaches of investment for anyone. Those who are most successful with this approach buy only when the market and individual stocks are quite depressed. They buy most of their stock during the last phases of reces-

sions and before prices and the tempo of buying have ac-
celerated. They select only the soundest stocks, based upon
fundamental values. These companies have shown a consistent
and steady growth of sales. Their pretax profits are expanding
as a percentage of sales, and their earnings-per-share have increased in each of the past three years and have topped the
average climb of firms in the Dow Jones Index. If these investors are looking for income in addition to appreciation, they
seek stocks that will give them a steady and growing return
on their original equity. They buy regularly and sell seldom.
This approach is one of the best for those who want to build
their net worth over a period of years.

MY APPROACH:
RAPID GROWTH, MINIMUM RISK

One of the things you soon discover is that different
experts don't have one system for selecting stocks. They have
a variety of systems. Some of these systems work better than
others. Most work when the whole market is going up. Fewer
work when the whole market is going down. But even in bear
markets, some investors consistently make money. This book
is written to help you be one of these. Even in bullish markets,
some people consistently lose. Buy high and sell low seems to
be their fate in life. Certainly, this book will help you part
company with this group.

The approach I'm discussing here is a rapid growth approach, but, if properly executed, one with minimum risk. *My
approach is based upon a very simple, sound, conservative, and
money-making philosophy: buy low-priced stocks based upon
their fundamental value.* That is, buy stocks which are underpriced, cheap, a bargain—in comparison to what they are really
worth or are going to be worth in a year's time.

Essentially, I am a conservative person. I don't like to take a chance if I can avoid it. I'd rather be certain of earning somewhat less money than to take a greater chance, even with the possibilities of earning more. My own approach to investing is essentially a conservative one, because it is based upon fundamental values. But I'm not so conservative that I buy stocks just to receive dividends (In times of high interest rates, I can make more from our money market funds.), nor do I want to wait five years to realize even a 50 percent profit (I can also do better than that elsewhere). I want to buy stock for only one reason: I can make more money faster through stocks than through other forms of investment. If I can't, I'm not interested in the market. Picking stocks, watching and keeping track of them, and buying and selling them, takes time and trouble. If I'm going to do it, I want it to pay off. If it doesn't, I'm not interested, especially if I can sock money away at 10 to 12 percent interest without ever having to worry about it.

I'm not saying that buying stocks—even the best of them —is never a gamble. It is. So many things can happen that influence the price of your stock, things over which you have absolutely no control. Interest rates can go up, a tendered offer can be withdrawn, a president can be assassinated or resign, war may break out, a company that had been promised a multibillion dollar defense contract can suddenly be denied it. Any one of these things, plus countless others, may influence the price of your stock. But by buying stocks based upon sound value, you minimize your risk on the down side and maximize your potential on the up side, and—in the long run—you're more likely to end up a winner.

How many times have you said: "If I just knew which stocks to buy, I could make a lot of money." And so you could. And so could everyone else. Because picking the winners is the key to making money in the market, more thought has been given to this subject than any other. Multimillion dollar companies spend millions hiring the finest analysts just to gain some advantage in picking winners. These companies spend millions more in hiring the finest brokers to sell their stocks to the public. Most of the time, these efforts pay off, but only for those who bother to obtain the information available.

Unfortunately, too many buyers consistently ignore most of these vast stores of information. They never bother to find out very much about any company before they purchase the stock. Or, they wrongly feel that learning how to select stocks is too complicated, so they never bother to try. I feel very strongly that this is not true. I feel that *the average investor can learn how to select low-priced, sound growth stocks that are good buys based upon their own individual characteristics and upon sound financial profiles of the companies they represent.* This book will tell you how.

3

TEN CONSIDERATIONS IN SELECTING STOCKS

A sound, conservative, growth approach to picking winning, low-priced stocks should take into consideration the following ten important factors.

1. The present price of the stock in relation to previous trends, highs, and lows.

2. The present price/earning ratio of the stock—this is the present price of the stock divided by the earnings per share over the past year—and the projected price/ earnings ratio in the coming year, or years, at the present-day price of the stock.

3. The earnings/share record of the company over the past several years, along with projections for the coming year or years.

4. Annual sales and profit figures and projections.

5. The financial health of the company as measured by current liabilities and by long-term indebtedness as a percentage of stockholder equity.

6. The book value of the stock compared to its price.

7. The prospects for the industry of which the company is a part over the next year or years.

8. Special features or facts about a particular company that give it unusual status within the industry or that will significantly affect its earning record in the year or years to come.

9. The status of the company in the investment community.
10. The trend of the whole stock market and the prospects over the next year as it relates to the national economy and the world situation.

Each of these factors will be discussed in turn.

STOCK PRICE

Resolve from the beginning that you are going to eliminate from consideration all stocks selling over $10 per share, no matter how attractive they may seem. Actually, I narrow the field down more than that. I ordinarily prefer stocks that are selling for no more than $6 to $8 per share. As a general rule, I try to buy stocks that are selling as cheaply as possible *provided they represent sound companies.* Other things being equal, I'd rather buy 1,000 shares of a $2 stock, than 200 shares of a $10 one, since one of my goals is to own as many shares as possible. Also, I like to diversify, so if I spend too much on one stock, I won't have as much money available to buy others or to average downward on ones I want to reenforce.

My suggestion would be to determine first how much money you want to invest. Is it several hundred dollars, a thousand, several thousand? You certainly don't want to put all of your money in one stock. And, if you're new at the game, start very moderately while you're learning.

Say you want to invest $1,000. Then buy 200 shares of a $2 stock and another 200 of a $3 one. The more money you have to invest, the greater the variety of stocks you can buy and the more you can pay per share.

You also have to look at the price trends on each individual stock. Is the stock selling high, low, or at a medium price in comparison with its price this year and prior years? If the stock is selling at its high for the year, be certain it's still a good buy at that price before purchasing. No stock keeps going up—it goes up and down—no matter how much of a bargain. If it already has had a fast upswing that seems to be leveling off, wait awhile to see if it's going to go down before you purchase. Obviously, you want to try to hit the lows. No one can do so all the time, so don't be upset if you don't. If you've made a good buy, it will go back up.

PRICE/EARNING (P/E) RATIOS

The P/E ratio is one measure of whether or not a stock is a good buy.

Try to buy low-priced stocks with P/E ratios of from 3 to 8. You may find occasional stocks with lower ratios than 3. Sometimes this is all right, but it may indicate some real problems with the company, so make a thorough investigation before you proceed.

Why am I suggesting P/E ratios of 3 to 8? Because these ratios give you a maximum potential for price increases on the upside and minimum risks of price declines on the downside. Ratios of 3 to 8 are considerably lower than those for stocks in general. Here were some typical ratios in 1981–1982.

Standard & Poor's 400 Industrials as of 1/31/81	9.2
Standard & Poor's 500 as of 5/25/82	7.5
Dow Jones Industrials for 12 months ended 3/31/82	8.4
Barron's 50 Stock Average as of 5/27/82	7.9

Since then, however, the P/E ratios have been rising as the rally continues. By June 1983, the P/E ratio of S & P 500 stocks had risen to 12.9. Barron's 50 Stock Average was 112.6. The average ratio rises and falls with the market. During rallies you may have to select stocks with much higher ratios than when the market is depressed. Figure 3.1 shows the trends in P/E ratios from 1968 to 1983, using the average ratios of S & P 500 stocks. Note the high was 20.4 in 1971; the low was 6.8 in 1979.

If you select stocks whose ratios are about one-half the average, the stock can double in price before it would be selling at an average price in relationship to earnings. Of course, different stocks have different averages. High technology stocks have very high ratios in comparison to averages. Some industry groups have low ratios when they are depressed (the oil exploration stocks would be a good example in 1983). But you can find out what averages are for particular industry groups and see how your stock compares to the average. By buying fast-growth stocks below market prices, you have the greatest opportunity to make maximum profits.

Companies whose earnings are growing very fast may have very high P/E ratios in anticipation of continued growth. But there always seems to be some companies that are growing fast, whose ratios have not yet caught up with their growth. These are the kinds of buys to look for, since the stocks are undervalued in price.

Even among the top 50 companies on the ASE, whose stock prices had already increased the most during 1981, the medium P/E ratio as of 12/31/81 was 10. (This means that half of these companies had P/E ratios below and half had ratios above that figure.) Interestingly, at the beginning of 1981, the medium P/E ratio of these same stocks was also 10. The stocks subsequently skyrocketed in price. But the earnings were also skyrocketing, so the medium P/E ratios for the

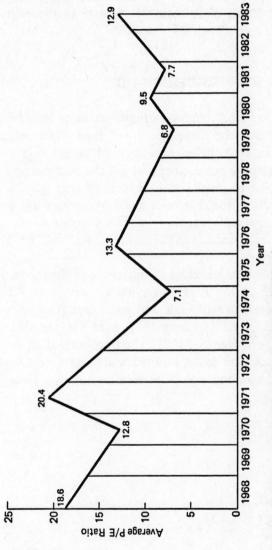

FIGURE 3.1 P/E RATIOS OF S & P 500 STOCKS

group remained the same. Other things being equal, a lower P/E ratio leaves more room for growth in the price of the stock than does a high P/E ratio.

EARNINGS PER SHARE

Select stocks whose earnings per share have been rising the fastest over the longest period of time. Thus, other things being equal, I would select a stock whose earnings per share have gone up 40 percent per year for the past three years over a stock whose earnings per share have gone up only 20 percent per year. Or, I would select a stock whose earnings per share have increased each year for four years over one whose earnings per share have increased the same amount but for only the past two years.

Let's take an actual example, one of the top performers on the ASE during 1981 and 1982: Greenman (GMN). The company deals in wholesale and retail toys. The price of this stock increased 82% during 1981, from 3½ per share to 6⅜ per share as of Dec. 31, 1981. The price leveled off for awhile and then took off again in 1982 and 1983 (see Chapter 5). The actual earnings per share were as follows, as of Jan. of each year:

1977	.13
1978	.15
1979	.32
1980	.75
1981	.92
1982	1.52

This is an increase in earnings/share of almost 1200 percent in five years, certainly an enviable record. In spite of the rapid price escalation, the stock was still selling for only 6.7 times its earnings as of June 1982, and 10 times its earnings as of June 1983.

Sometimes, earnings of a company are on the rebound after being depressed for several years. Let's take another example from among the top 50 performers on the ASE during 1981 and 1982: Caressa, Inc. (CSA), manufacturer and importer of shoes. The price of the stock increased from $3 per share to 5¼ per share during 1981, for a 75 percent appreciation. As of June 2, 1982, the stock had continued to increase in price to 8⅝ per share, and was still selling for only 5 times its earnings. By June 1983, the high had been 23⅜ per share, just a little over 10 times its earnings! The earnings per share have been as follows (including extraordinary charges):

1978	.40
1979	.19
1980	.16
1981	.74
1982	2.02

It is quite obvious that after two years of decline in earnings, the company turned around sharply and made a dramatic rise. The rapid increase in the price of the stock partly reflected the rise.

This does not mean that stock prices always follow earnings changes exactly. Stock prices may lag behind earnings (a good time to buy), or may anticipate earnings rises and be ahead of them (in which case caution should be exercised). But, in the long run, earnings' trends certainly do influence stock prices. Sometimes you have to wait for stock prices to catch up with earnings or for earnings to catch up with stock prices. If you can get projections of earnings for months ahead, you can make even more intelligent guesses as to what the price of the stock may do.

SALES AND PROFIT FIGURES

Other things being equal, you want to invest in companies whose annual sales and pretax profits as a percentage of sales are increasing as rapidly as possible. If the volume of goods sold is increasing, and the pretax profits are increasing even more, not only is the company expanding its business, but it is operating more efficiently as time goes on. A company that increases its volume of business but has static profits is either facing negative market conditions over which it has little control or is not being well managed. Either condition will tend to depress the price of the stock.

Sometimes earnings-per-share figures are distorted by extraordinary circumstances: tax write-offs that are carried forward from a previous year, profits from sales of part of the company assets, a heavy investment in new plants or equipment, or other extraordinary income or expenses. When you read earnings-per-share figures, be sure to read any footnotes in conjunction with them that indicate extraordinary charges or income. If earnings figures seem inflated or deflated, referring to actual figures on sales volume and pretax profits will enable you to tell whether the business of the company is growing or declining.

When conglomerates first became popular, companies that merged with others would often show very inflated earnings/share figures (not taking into account stock dilution). New regulations finally forced them to adjust their accounting practices to present a more realistic picture. Also, earnings figures should take into account any stock splits, dilution of earnings/share by issuance of additional stocks, or improved earnings/share by a company buying up part of its own stock. Here again, sales volume and profit figures are indicators of actual business trends of the company.

COMPANY HEALTH

There are various ways of judging the financial health of a company. The most important figures are current assets in relation to current liabilities. Unless current assets at least equal current liabilities, the company can't pay its bills the coming month without temporary financing, unless the cash shortage is temporary. In the healthiest situation current assets should be twice the current liabilities. In other words, the ratio of current assets to current liabilities is 2:1. If possible, try to buy stocks in companies that approximate this ratio. This may not always be possible, especially in companies that are expanding very rapidly and continually putting their cash back into company investments. But at least you know what accountants consider ideal. Whether or not you can always find this is a question.

It is important also to look at long-term indebtedness in relationship to stockholder equity. Stockholder equity is the book value (not market value) per share of stock "times" the number of shares outstanding. Thus, if a stock has a book value of $10 per share and a million shares are outstanding, the stockholder's equity is 10 million dollars. If the long-term indebtedness is exactly equal to the stockholder's equity, a ratio of 1:1, the company would barely be able to pay its indebtedness if it liquidated.

Of course, the amount of a company's indebtedness will

determine the amount of its total earnings that will be required to pay the interest charges and the principals of its loans. However, a company that has no indebtedness at all may not be expanding, renewing old equipment, or spending money to keep up-to-date. So, there is a happy medium. A conservative approach would say that the long-term debt should be less than 35 percent of the total stockholder's equity, especially in days of high interest rates. This is an ideal, but it deserves careful consideration. Indebtedness is only one of many factors to consider when evaluating the financial health of a company. More detailed information is given in Chapter 4.

BOOK VALUE

Book value is the assigned value per share of stock on the company balance sheets. It is an accounting figure and is not the same as the market price-per-share of stock.

Other things being equal, *if the stock is selling below book value per share, it is a better buy than if it is selling at or above book value.* Actually, book value usually has very little to do with the price of a stock. The reason is that most investors don't know what the book value is and don't even bother to find out. They're more concerned with earnings. However, book value is one more figure to take into consideration in trying to determine whether you're making a good buy or not.

PROSPECTS
FOR THE INDUSTRY

Business goes in cycles, but some industries are more cyclical than others. They have good years and bad years, and their performance varies. Other industries are less cyclical, but even they show variations in performance. It is important to remember that the performance of all industries is not the same during any one year. So once you have found some stocks you like, you have to determine the prospects for the industries of which your stocks are a part. The reason is that the stock prices usually reflect or try to predict these industrial fluctuations. There's no point in buying a stock in an industry that is still undergoing a significant downturn, unless you have the patience to wait until the turn around, which may take several years. I like to buy when prices are down but after they have already started back up. Usually, prices will appreciate faster in these kinds of situations.

Most brokerage houses and investment advisory services publish volumes of information giving guidance on those industries they feel are going to do well in the coming year and those that are going to do poorly. Remember though, these standings change from year to year. So you have to be flexible. Don't stay with any one industry all the time. Change with the market and you'll do better.

SPECIAL FEATURES OR
FACTS ABOUT A COMPANY

Try to find out as much as possible about an individual company, with the emphasis on special features or facts that give a company unusual status within an industry or that will significantly affect its earning record in the year to come. For example, does the company have a patent on a new or unusual product that is not available from other companies? A recent example is Key Pharmaceuticals (KPH), a Miami based firm that is finding time-release ways of administering old drugs.

They have developed *Theo-Dur,* a pill containing a 50-year-old anti-asthma drug, theophylline, that releases the medicine into the blood stream in equal doses over a 12-hour period. They have also introduced *Nitro-Dur,* a patch worn on the skin, that releases nitroglycerin in the bloodstream over a 24 hour period. The patch has been a blessing to angina sufferers, since it not only eases their pain, but also prevents attacks. For awhile, Key Pharmaceuticals was the only company with this product. As a result, the stock rose from a low of 5⅞ in 1980 to a 1983 high of 35⅛, with an astronomical P/E ratio of 69. I am offering this example not as a buy recommendation but as an illustration of how one company profited from introducing a product that no one else was making. Other companies are now scrambling to put out similar products.

There are countless special features to look for: a radical change in company management which is drastically improving its operations, a spin-off of a deficit-ridden section of a company, obtaining or losing a government contract that affects earnings, the take-over of a company by another firm, a significant find by a natural resource company, or an unusually healthy or unhealthy financial condition. Any one of these factors, along with countless others, can affect stock prices.

I also try to avoid companies that are too small. (I would consider sales of less than 25 million dollars a year small. In comparison, the largest 1000 industrial companies in the United States each had 1981 sales of $122.5 million or more.) Companies that are too small don't attract as much national attention for investors. Also, if they have small capitalization, with very few shares changing hands, there is often less demand to drive the price of the stock up. Therefore, you need to read as much as you can about individual companies. This will determine whether the purchase of their stock is a good or bad buy.

STATUS OF A COMPANY IN THE INVESTMENT COMMUNITY

There are numerous ways of determining this status. One way is by using the rankings given by Standard and Poor in their monthly issue of the *Stock Guide*. They rank stocks as follows:

A+	Highest	B	Below Average
A	High	B—	Lower
A—	Above Average	C	Lowest
B+	Average	D	In Reorganization

These rankings are primarily based on the degree of growth and stability of earnings and dividends based upon the most recent 10 years. These rankings are not a forecast of future market prices, but of past performance, so they can't be used alone as a prediction of what stocks are going to do in the future. Also, the ranking emphasizes stability more than rapid growth, so they are not the best indicators of best-buys in rapid growth stocks. The rankings also tend to favor the largest corporations and, as such, are not the best guides to buying low-priced stocks.

Another way of determining the status of a stock in the investment community is by the number of institutions holding shares, and the number of shares held by them. If institutions buy the shares, the stock is presumably held in higher regard than those not purchased by them. However, sometimes too many shares are held by institutions, so many, in fact, that the institutions have too great an influence on the price of the stock. Or, when a lot of shares are held by only a few companies, the price of the stock goes down if the institutions sell. A general guideline is to look for stocks that are owned by institutions, but where not more than 10 percent of the total capitalization is owned by them. Or, look for stocks that are suddenly being bought by institutions. There are usually good reasons for the popularity of such stocks. Let's use Key Pharmaceuticals as an example again. At the end of 1979, only three institutions owned 51,000 shares of this stock out of a total capitalization of 4,970,000. By the end of 1980, those figures had risen to 10 institutions owning 545,000 shares out of 8,707,000. By the end of 1981, 13 institutions owned 958,000 shares out of 15,155,000. By the end of 1982, 43 institutions owned 3,103,000 shares out of 23,076,000. After this time, institutions began reducing their holdings somewhat.

Let's also take just the opposite example: Braniff International Airlines (BNF), which recently filed for bankruptcy. Braniff had a rosy picture of growing earnings through 1978. In January 1979, the stock was selling for over $12 per share. Earnings then fell drastically from $2.26 per share in 1978 to a deficit of $2.21/share in 1979. Here's what happened—earnings are reflected in stock prices and institutional holdings.

TABLE 3.1
Braniff International (BNF)

YEAR	EARNINGS/ SHARE	STOCK PRICE AT END OF YEAR	INSTITUTIONAL HOLDINGS		TOTAL CAPITAL- IZATION
			No. Companies	*Shares Held*	
1979	−$2.21	8½	67	7,276,000	20 million
1980	− 6.57	5	53	6,121,000	20 million
1981	− 6.22	2¼	21	973,000	20 million

As seen in Table 3.1, over ⅓ of the common stock in 1979 was owned by institutions. A surprising number of institutions held onto their shares, even through the two years of increasing deficits—until the end of 1980. Undoubtedly, some new institutions bought in, thinking that a turn-around was imminent and believing that buying at such a low price would pay off. (This is a good lesson to learn: wait until after a turn-around to buy, not before.) By the end of 1980, the institutions were finally convinced that the deficits were not going to be corrected and began unloading as the stock fell to 2¼. In this case, the continued extensive ownership by institutions probably kept the price of the stock up much longer than it deserved.

This example also illustrates the point that the institutions are not always right; however, their actions can give you additional information in deciding whether or not to buy or sell. Because of their large holdings, institutions aren't as agile as an individual in getting in and out of the market.

Probably the best indicators of the status of stocks in the investment community are the *buy* and *sell* recommendations of the major brokerage houses, investment analysts, and investment advisory services. Some individuals and some companies are so influential that they can influence stock prices simply on the basis of their *buy* and *sell* recommendations. Their recommendations then become self-fulfilling prophecies. What these persons and companies say is not always right, but what they say does have influence, so you ought to get as much information from as many different sources as possible. If you are thinking of purchasing a stock, check it out with several brokerage houses to see what they have to say about it. If no one has issued a report on it and you are still interested, you have to use your best judgment.

A word of caution: Don't buy just because a friend or relative recommends the stock, or even because your broker says to buy it, without checking out its fundamental value yourself. You're paying for the stock, and you alone will bear the consequences of your decisions. You should make enlightened, informed decisions. If you've studied the stock and its company for some time, chances are that you have much more intimate knowledge of it than the average broker. If, however, you get a buy recommendation on a low-priced, rapid growth stock from an expert analyst, you certainly should at least listen and take the recommendation into consideration along with other factors.

THE TREND OF THE MARKET

If possible, take into account market trends in buying and selling. If the whole market is going up, the best stocks go up the most, and the worst stocks go up the least (if they go up at all). If the whole market is going down, the worst stocks decline the most, and the best stocks decline the least (if they decline at all). If the whole market has declined, the best stocks are poised, ready to increase rapidly, as soon as the turnaround comes. If the whole market has peaked, and a turnaround occurs, the worst stocks will decline the soonest and fastest. Correct timing is one key to successful investing, but also one of the hardest skills to develop. When J. P. Morgan, the great financier, was asked what the market was going to do, his candid reply was: "It's going to fluctuate." That is probably the most that can be said with absolute certainty.

Even though hundreds of experts study market trends to try to predict what the market is going to do, they have been wrong so often that their opinions are only one factor to consider when buying stock. If the experts do not agree, and often they do not, you're in a dilemma. In such cases, I would seek out only the most professional opinion. One such professional is Newton Zinder, a technical market analyst with E. F. Hutton. When he speaks, people listen. Another such professional is Robert Farrell, chief market analyst of Merrill, Lynch, Pierce, Fenner, and Smith. He was voted the outstanding market analyst in the United States each year for six years, 1976–1981, in a row. He is the kind of person whose advice you ought to seek.

Certainly, as lay people, all we can do is get the best opinions possible, and, when it comes right down to it we still have to use our own judgment. It's not disastrous if you don't hit the exact bottom—no one always does—if you have bought a sound stock. Some stocks are so good that they are good buys most of the time. Some stocks are so poor they are bad buys no matter when you purchase them.

4

PICKING
WINNERS
STEP-BY-STEP

Over the years, I've developed a system of selecting low-priced stocks that has worked for me. I have never lost money on any stocks that I have selected by using this system. I have made very high returns on many of them. This doesn't mean that none of the stocks has ever gone below its purchase price. Some have, but usually on a temporary basis. In the long run, all have ended up winners.

My system is based upon the ten considerations discussed in the previous chapter. But in this chapter, I want to suggest a step-by-step procedure for stock selection by taking these ten important factors into account. The system enables you to find and select your stocks yourself, relying on professional help as needed. It's not a matter of calling your broker and asking: What stocks shall I buy? In fact, I've had brokers recommend my selections to their clients after I have found the stocks. My system is a search-and-find method that can be done with speed and efficiency but that still requires some time and effort. Personally, I think it's a lot of fun. And it's a challenge to beat the market and come out a winner.

STEP ONE

Decide whether you're going to start with stocks on the NYSE, the ASE, or OTC stocks as quoted by the National Association of Security Dealers Automated Quotations (NASDAQ). During times of recession, you may find many low-priced stocks on the NYSE. If you can find them, the NYSE is a good place to begin. However, there are a few low-priced stocks on the big board that have been at their present level for years for one reason—they're not growing, expanding companies. Try to avoid these companies.

During more prosperous times, you'll find very few low-priced stocks on the NYSE, so you'll have to switch to the ASE and the OTC. I really prefer the ASE to OTC stocks, although the latter has some of the newest, fastest-growing companies.

The major reason I dislike OTC quotations is that the newspapers never list the P/E ratios for each stock, so I have to look these up separately for each stock—an inconvenience. Therefore, I start with the NYSE and the ASE, and then buy OTC stocks if I can't find what I'm looking for on the other two exchanges.

STEP TWO

After selecting an exchange, use Barron's *National Business and Financial Weekly* or other sources of weekly composite figures such as the *Wall Street Journal,* and go through the entire list, checking off those stocks that are in the price category you are looking for (but no more than $10 per share) and with P/E ratios of 8 or lower. Obviously, the more you're willing to pay per share, the longer your list. So you might start with the cheapest stocks first: say those which are $2–6/ share with P/E ratios of 3–6. These restrictions will narrow down your list considerably. If you can't find enough prospects from these restrictions, raise the maximum price you're willing to pay per share or the maximum P/E ratio you're looking for. If your list is too long, lower the maximum price you're willing to pay per share and/or lower the maximum P/E ratio to 3–5, or 3–4. However, this is seldom possible when the whole market is high. It's helpful at this stage to have a couple dozen prospects.

STEP THREE

Using Standard and Poor's *Stock Guide,* look up the earnings-per-share records of each of your prospects for the last five years. Barron's *National Business and Financial Weekly* also lists the latest interim or fiscal years earnings, but not the records of previous years. The very latest interim-earnings reports are particularly important since they give you the latest trends as compared with last year. Obviously, those companies whose earnings are rising the fastest and longest are the best prospects, based upon earnings alone (there are, of course, many other important considerations too).

You can't find many companies whose earnings have gone up consistently and rapidly for five years. But look for these to see if you can find them. Also, remember that earnings have to be rising faster than inflation, or else the company is not showing earnings gains in real terms. Earnings increases of 8 percent in an economy with an inflation rate of 10 percent is actually a very poor showing. You need to look for real rapid growth.

Also, look for turn-around situations, where earnings may have declined but have been on the rise again. The longer the rise has been sustained, the better. Increases in earnings for less than a year may not be important, unless they indicate a much improved situation that may be sustained over a longer period of time. Investors often wait to see if increases are only temporary or permanent. At this stage, you may want to rank your stocks based upon earnings records, indicating which ones are not quite as attractive, and so forth, right down the list, eliminating the weakest ones from further consideration.

STEP FOUR

Using Standard and Poor's *Stock Guide* or other sources (see Chapter 12), make preliminary investigations of the financial status and health of the company. Look first at current assets in relation to current liabilities. Which companies have ratios of 2:1 or greater? Which ones are less? The higher the ratio, the more liquid the company's position. Rate the companies according to liquidity.

You may also want to look at the figures on *yield*—percentage returns on your investments in the form of dividends. I haven't said much about yield, since I don't select stocks for their dividends. Some of the fastest growing companies don't pay any dividends at all. I'd rather have a stock appreciate in price by 30 to 40 percent than one that has little or no appreciation and receives a dividend of 10 percent. However, if you're looking for income in addition to appreciation, you'll want to take yield into account. Obviously, if I can earn some dividends as well as money from appreciation, then so much the better.

Sometimes you can find companies that have just announced a stock split or a sizable stock dividend that is payable to those holding stock on a record date that is forthcoming. Such announcements usually increase the price of the stock on a temporary basis and may be one factor to consider when thinking of purchasing the stock.

STEP FIVE

Continue your investigations of the financial health and status of your prospects, as represented by total revenue, net income before taxes, net income as a percentage of rev-

enue, book value versus market price, and long-term debt as a
percentage of stockholders' equity. One best way of obtaining
this information is to ask your broker for photocopies of
Standard and Poor's *Stock Reports* or Moody's *Investors Fact
Sheets* for each company on your prospect list. These brief
reports are the single best source of financial and descriptive
reports on the companies you are interested in. Look for the
following data (items are numbered for reference here):

1. Total revenue figures each quarter for the past 5 years.
2. Total net income before taxes for each of the past 5
   years.
3. No. of shares of common stock outstanding.
4. Book value per share of common stock.
5. Shareholders' equity (#3 × #4 value).
6. Total long-term debt.

Check the total revenue figures (1) first. Chances are that if
your list includes only those stocks whose earnings per share are
increasing, revenues for each quarter will also be increasing.

If they aren't, the improved earnings are being ac-
complished not by an improvement in sales but by reducing
costs or from extraordinary income from other sources. Other
things being equal, the best companies should be showing
maximum increases in revenues. Then check out total net income before taxes (2). These figures should also be increasing.
Now, divide total net income by total revenue for each year
(2 divided by 1). Is total net income as a percentage of the
total revenue increasing? Companies that are improving operating efficiency show increases.

Next, look up the latest figures for book value (4).
At the present price of the stock, is the stock selling below, at,
or above book value? A stock is more likely to be a safe buy

if it is selling below book value, but this figure is not as important as some of the others.

Next, examine the figures for total stockholders' equity (5) and long-term debt (6), and calculate long-term debt as a percentage of stockholders' equity (6 divided by 5) for each year. The soundest companies are those whose long-term debts are no more than 35 percent of the stockholders' equity.

If the Standard and Poor's *Stock Report* is more than three months old, look up the latest information in Standard and Poor's *Corporation Records* (found in every major brokerage house) or Moody's *Bi-weekly News Reports* to see if reports on the company are available. These cumulative records contain daily, weekly, and biweekly reports and news items on corporations. You can look up your companies in the index sections. Have your broker photocopy those pages that apply to the companies you are investigating. This latest information is helpful in evaluating up-to-date financial operations of each company. Look for up-to-date quarterly revenue and net-income-before-taxes figures. Also, see if there are any special financial announcements included: announcements of a dividend or stock split, issuance of more stock, or increases in indebtedness. You need to be concerned about any and all facts relating to the financial health of the companies you are investigating.

STEP SIX

The next step is to discover special features or facts about a company that give it an unusual status in the industry or facts that are likely to affect its prospects in the next year or so. The Standard and Poor's *Stock Reports* and *Corporation Records* and Moody's *Manuals, Investors Fact Sheets* and *New Reports* not only contain financial figures, but also contain descriptive information about each company: what services or products the company sells, the company's position in the industry, recent developments, and prospects for the future. These data will enable you to get a much broader picture of company operations than you get from the financial data. The *Corporation Records* and *News Reports* include the quarterly, semiannual, and annual reports that are published by the companies themselves. These reports reflect the management's appraisal of the present situation and the prospects for the future. You need to know what they are thinking.

STEP SEVEN

Try to find out the prospects for the industries of which your companies are a part. Which industries are expected to do well or poorly in the year ahead? Obviously, try to select companies in the industries that are expected to do the best. The more you read about stocks, the more information you will glean from a variety of sources about prospects for different industries.

STEP EIGHT

Find out what the investment community thinks of your prospects. By this time, you will have learned a great deal about each company whose stock you are contemplating buying. After you have done all of this investigation yourself, you should make a determined effort to get the opinions of experts in relation to individual stocks. Begin by looking up the Standard and Poor rankings in the *Stock Guide*. (See the discussion of these rankings in the previous chapter.) Next, look up the number of institutions holding shares and the number of shares held (see the *Stock Guide*). These figures will give you some additional information about the status of the stock in the investment community. I prefer to buy stocks that are held by some institutions. However, if too many shares are held by institutions (over 10 percent of capitalization), it may indicate an undue influence of those institutions on the price of this stock.

Call a number of different brokerage houses and ask each of them if their analysts have any reports on the companies on your list. Ask them to send you the reports they have available. Also ask them for computer printouts that summarize information they keep in their computer bank. Ask them if they know of any reports on any of your companies from any of the investment advisory services, in business and trade journals, popular magazines, or in daily or weekly newspapers. Sometimes a broker will remember an article you have not seen. The idea is to get as much additional information on your companies as you can glean from professional sources.

STEP NINE

Narrow down your list by eliminating the poorest prospects and by ranking the others in the order in which you want to buy. I would, however, always keep more stocks on my list than I could afford to purchase immediately. This way selections were already made when money became available.

STEP TEN

Decide if you want to buy now or wait until a more appropriate time. In making this decision, you must consider the price trends of each stock, you must decide if it's at its high, low, or medium price, and you must formulate an idea of what you think the price is going to do in the immediate future. You also must consider the trend of the whole market, which certainly will have some effects on what individual stocks will do. If you're uncertain about the stock price and the timing of your purchase, watch it awhile, or buy only part of the shares now and buy additional ones later if the price goes down. See Chapter 5 on "When to Buy" and Chapter 6 on "Averaging Downward."

5

WHEN TO BUY

Once you have decided what stocks to buy, your next decision is when to execute the order to buy. This is a very important decision, because it determines, partially, how much money you are going to make and how long you will have to wait to make it. You can make money on any stock on any exchange by buying it at its low for the year and selling at its high. Some stocks are more volatile than others, evidenced by wide variations in price. Others are more stable, showing only slight changes. But all stock prices move, allowing you to make a profit if you can correctly time when to buy and when to sell.

Are there any rules or principles to go by? Yes, there are, and it is these I will discuss here.

MARKET TRENDS

Rule #1: You have a greater chance of making the most money rapidly by buying after the entire market has bottomed out and after it has signaled a turn-around and is on the uptrend. Falling volume usually indicates a declining market. If the volume stays low, this generally indicates continuing low prices. In this case, you may need to wait a while longer before buying.

If the decline has taken place over a period of time, has leveled off, and now the pace of buying has started to pick up, this may be an indication that the market has bottomed out and is starting to go up. The more the volume increases, and the longer stock prices go up, the more the market is confirming that it has become "bullish." In such cases, you need to jump in as early in the rally as possible to get in on rising prices.

The mistake many buyers make is they wait too long to buy after the market starts going up. In fact, many buy when the market is already at its peak. Excitement grows as the rally continues, bringing in more and more investors. This stimulates the rise even more. By the time many amateur investors decide to make a move, the rally is over, and they buy just in time to see their stock prices decline.

Rule #2: Buy when the whole market is in an uptrend and not when it is in a downtrend. There may be some exceptions to this, but it is usually unwise to try to buck the trend of the market. Only the strongest stocks will do so. If you're unsure about the market trend, consult the technical experts in the major brokerage houses. They'll advise you about short, intermediate, and long-term trends.

Rule #3: If you're going to invest in stocks on a regular basis, do so during uptrends or after stock prices are already depressed and fairly static, saving your money during downtrends or when the market is already high. General activity may be minimal when prices are depressed, but, if you continue to buy stocks at depressed prices, when a rally develops, you will have significant holdings from which you can reap maximum profits. This method, of course, takes time. You have to be able to hold onto your stocks while you weather the storm, confident that a rally is ahead. The real advantage to this method is that you have a longer period to buy—during the bottom of a recession in many instances—so once prices start going up, you stand to make a considerable amount of money.

What about monthly investment when the whole market is at a peak? You're usually better off salting your money in other income-producing, fairly liquid investments during peak months, waiting for temporary or longer term declines to bottom out before jumping in. There are exceptions to this (when you find individual stocks that are underpriced, lagging behind the general rally, and only starting to increase in price). But we're talking in general about whole market trends. The general rule holds: Buy when prices are rising, or are depressed, but not when they are falling or are at their peak.

Rule #4: The market is usually about six months ahead of shifts in the economy, so take this into account in timing purchases. Thus, the rally of 1982–1983 began in August 1982, but the economy did not see any significant improvement until the spring of 1983. If a buyer had waited until the economy had already improved, the major rally in stock prices would have already been over.

Similarly, declines in stock prices precede recessions, so the time to sell is when stock prices start to decline, not after a recession has already happened. Thus, the decline in stock prices started in the Spring of 1981, long before the government confirmed that we were in a recession. Unemployment at the time was still only 7 percent. Industrial production and new orders for durable goods did not start to decline until after the middle of 1981.

Since the market anticipates what the economy is going to do, rather than the other way around, use the market action as your primary guide, rather than economic indicators. During the Spring of 1983, the economy continued to improve, but stock prices were already leveling off, so experts were urging caution in buying. Major issues had already finished running up; the only good buys were the lesser known companies that were just beginning to respond or that were enjoying continual fast-earnings growth.

Generally speaking, primary issues lead a rally, while secondary issues respond later on. The longer a rally goes on, the harder it becomes to find good buys, and the more you'll have to look at the smaller, lesser known companies. You often can still make handsome profits, but you'll have to search and to exercise more caution in your selections.

INDIVIDUAL STOCK PRICES

Rule #5: Buy an individual stock only if it is a good buy at that price and not just because the whole market is bullish. Poor choices won't make the maximum money in any kind of market. If you select your individual stocks according to the criteria I've outlined, you're going to make the most money possible in a bull market, and you're more likely to make money in a bear market.

Rule #6: Buy individual stocks on the basis of anticipated market performance, not on the basis of past performance. It's very easy to go through a list of stocks and select the ones that have already appreciated the most. But just because a stock has already doubled in price does not mean it is going to continue doing so. It may have reached its peak and is in for a significant decline, especially if earnings have not kept up with the stock price, if it is selling at a high P/E ratio, and if the prospects for sales in the months and quarters ahead are not bright.

Most buyers feel safer jumping on the band wagon and buying the issues that are very popular at the moment. It's a very real temptation to buy such stocks. You learn that your next door neighbor has made a lot of money on stock X. He tells you, "you better buy it, and share in the profits." But by the time you do, the rally is over, he sells, and you're stuck with stock that is already declining in price.

The solution, of course, is to buy in anticipation of rising prices. How do you do this? By selecting those companies whose stocks are selling at very low P/E ratios, whose sales, profits, and earnings per share are rising rapidly, that are financially sound, and that have bright prospects for the future. In other words, by selecting stocks according to the criteria I've outlined. Get projections of future sales, profits, and earnings, and buy those stocks that are already undervalued according to these projections.

But you say, the price of stock Y hasn't gone up much. Not too many investors are buying it. Not yet, but they will if the stock is as good as you think it is. You can buy now and sit back and smile when it starts to move, or you can watch it carefully, jumping in the moment that volume and price start to increase. I've watched some stocks for months or even for over a year until—bingo—the rally starts. If it was extremely underpriced, it might go up for months or even for a number of years before hitting an unbelievable high! And it's a real satisfaction to get in on the ground floor—before most investors have even realized it existed.

What about buying stocks that have already enjoyed a significant advance? The same rule applies to them as to any stock. Buy such stocks only if they are now superior buys according to their anticipated performance in the future. The fact that they have already increased significantly in price should make you cautious, but this alone is not a good enough reason not to buy them, especially if they are still undervalued on the basis of P/E ratios, company sales, profits, and earnings in the months ahead.

Let's take two examples already discussed in Chapter 3 of this book: Greenman Brothers (GMN) and Caressa, Inc. (CSA), both listed on the Amex, both superior performers during 1981. Greenman went up 82 percent during 1981 and Caressa went up 75 percent.

Greenman leveled off to 6⅛ as of June 2, 1982, but was still selling at a P/E ratio of only 6.7. Earnings projections for 1982 were around $1.25 per share. If the stock increased to a price representing only 7 times the earnings, it should go up to at least 8¾, a rise of 43 percent. This was clearly still a very good buy. As it happened, the high for 1982 was 10⅜, but it subsequently dropped, ending the year at 8¾, with a P/E ratio of 7 based upon 12 months earnings at the end of October of $1.27 per share.

What has it done so far in 1983? The high so far has been 20⅛: It closed at 19¾ on May 27, still with a P/E ratio of only 10 times the earnings. As it happened, Greenman (which sells toys) had a better than anticipated last quarter, so that earnings/share for the fiscal year ending Jan. 1983 was $1.52 per share. Apparently, earnings are still going up and the stock price is increasing along with it.

What about Caressa? As of June 2, 1982, the stock had continued to increase in price to 8⅝ per share and was still selling for only 5 times the earnings. The projected earnings for 1982 was $2.02/share. At only 7 times the earnings, the projected price would be 14. As it happened, the stock earned exactly $2.02 per share in 1982 and closed in Dec. 1982, at 14. Since then, the high for 1983 has been 23⅜ per share! The stock has fallen some and closed on May 27, 1983 at 17¼, but still with only 8.5 times the earnings. Barron's reports the earnings for six months ending March 1983 of $1.01/share versus $.66 a year ago, so the earnings are still going up.

These examples are given to show that even though some stocks have appreciated significantly in price, they may still be good buys if their earnings continue to rise and they are still selling at reasonable multiples. Caressa was a turnaround situation. It closed in 1980 with a deficit and was selling for $3/share. With earnings turning around and skyrocketing, the stock increased in price almost 8 times the original price in 2½ years! Greenman has shown a rapid rise in earnings for the past 'five years. It closed at 3½ in Dec. of 1980, selling at 8 times the earnings and increased in value almost 6 times the original price during 2½ years. So don't neglect to look at stocks that have already increased in price. They may still be good values.

Rule #7: Once you've selected a stock, take advantage of short-term fluctuations in its price, buying during temporary declines. How do you pin-point these? One way I know of doing this is to watch it over a period of weeks. Record daily prices during this time. You'll soon get a feel for how the stock behaves. You'll know that a particular price is considerably below or above what the stock usually sells for. You'll recognize declines when they occur, so you can jump in at auspicious moments. This is especially important in low-priced stocks selling for $10 or less because variations of only one point represent changes of 10 percent or more. Proper timing can help you increase your profits.

Another way to learn about the actions of a stock is to get a chart on it, so you can see what it has been doing during previous weeks or months. Pay attention to the most recent high or low. How does the present price compare with these? No stock keeps going up-up-up without dips downward along the way. The reason is that investors who have already made good profits start selling, driving the price downward, until these prices become attractive enough for others to start buying.

What do you do if the price keeps going up while

you're watching the stock and before you've bought it? If the price has already appreciated, and you're convinced it's going to continue going up, buy the stock at that price—but only if it represents sound value according to the criteria I've outlined. Sometimes a stock moves up so fast and far that it becomes overpriced before you even have a chance to acquire it. In this case, forget it. Go on to another one. Never set your heart on buying just one stock. If you do, you'll be tempted to pay too much for it.

Another way of taking advantage of short-term fluctuations is to execute a buy order at a price that you feel is reasonable. If the stock dips to that price, you'll get it. Otherwise, you won't. This way, you don't have to watch it closely and worry each day about whether to buy it at that time. Some buyers place a number of buy orders at once. Some they get, some they don't. As long as all are good buys, it doesn't really matter. If you want to make sure that you buy a particular stock, you'll have to put in a purchase order at a high enough price to be certain you'll get it.

Rule #8: Other things being equal, buy a stock that has a greater volume of activity over one that shows less activity. This is true, however, only if, in other respects, they are equally good buys. I would not let trading volume alone be the consideration in stock selection. I've already said that the best buys often occur when prices are depressed and trading is slow or only starting to pick up. However, by purchasing a stock whose trading volume is greater than that of another stock, you are more likely to be able to sell it, and the superior volume is more likely to force the price of the stock up. If no one is buying a stock, it can never appreciate in price. If it is a good one, it will eventually be discovered, but it may take longer to go up than one that is already showing some activity.

Rule #9: Buy a stock under special circumstances only if you're sure that by so doing you're guaranteed a profit. Special circumstances include such things as announcements of special dividends, stock splits, tender offers by other companies, extraordinarily favorable earnings reports, and so on. Such announcements often stimulate a sudden rise in price, usually on only a short-term basis. If you buy as soon after the announcement as possible, you may get in early enough to make a quick profit. Most often, however, by the time the average investor gets the news, the stock's reaction is already over.

Never buy on the basis of rumor: because it is rumored that a stock is a take-over candidate or because it is rumored that such and such a company is going to make a tender offer. Most such rumors never materialize. You buy, and you're left waiting, waiting, waiting for definite news that never materializes. Therefore, buy only when such rumors have been definitely confirmed, and only after official action has taken place.

6

AVERAGING DOWNWARD

HOW IT WORKS

One way to minimize losses and to maximize profits on a stock that declines in price after you have purchased it is to average downward—that is, to buy some more of it after its price declines. Let's see how this works. Commission rates will be omitted for the sake of simplicity.

Suppose you buy 500 shares of stock Z at $7 per share. It subsequently declines to $6 per share. If after investigation, you're still convinced it's a good buy (based upon sound facts, not just hope), buy 500 more shares. Your total investment is:

500 shares @ $7/share	$3,500
500 shares @ $6/share	3,000
	$6,500

The stock has to go up only one-half point, to $6\frac{1}{2}$, before you break even (omitting commissions). If it goes back up to $7 per share, your profit is $500, a 7.7 percent profit.

Now let's suppose that after you buy the 500 shares @ $6 per share the stock continues downward to $5/share. You should reinvestigate the stock to try to discover any overlooked reasons for the decline. If you're convinced (based upon facts) that the stock is still an exceptionally good buy, buy 500 more shares @ $5/share (for a total of $2,500). Your total investment in the stock is now $9,000 and you own 1500 shares. The stock now has to go back up to $6 before you break even. If it goes back up to $7 per share, you make a profit of $1,500, or 17.8 percent (less commissions). Any appreciation in the stock above $7/share represents that much more profit. If it goes up to $8 per share, you make $3,000, or 33⅓ percent! Not bad on an original investment of only $9,000. If you had decided to sit tight with your original investment of 500 shares @ $7/share, your profit would have been only $500, or 14.3 percent.

Of course, the success of this method depends upon your stock moving back up in the near future. If it never goes back up at all, or continues downward, you never make a profit, and your losses multiply. This is why you should investigate the stock in question thoroughly before adding money to an original investment. If your search discloses facts that were heretofore not known to you that make your stock an unwise investment, not only should you not buy any more, but you would be well-advised to sell what you have already purchased, even at a loss. (See Chapter 7 on "When to Sell.")

ADVANTAGES
OVER BUYING NEW STOCKS

But you say, instead of putting more money in a stock you already own, one that has already declined, why not put new money into a completely different stock? In some cases, this may be the wisest move, but only if the new stock has better potential than the one you have already purchased. So make sure this is the case before you buy the new stock.

The advantage of purchasing some of the old stock is that presumably you have been following it closely and you have a better idea of its worth and of what it's going to do than you would if you bought a new one. It's entirely possible to purchase a new stock, or even several new ones, only to see them all decline in price after your purchase. This is not uncommon in a sustained bear market. Of course, you should not be buying then anyhow, but the market may have turned bearish after your purchases. So you're stuck with paper losses on all of them and have to wait until the whole market turns around before you can even recoup any of your losses. This may require some time. If you averaged downward, you would not have to wait as long to break even after the turnaround occurs and, once it happened, your chances of profit would be greater.

AVERAGING UPWARD

What about averaging upward, that is, buying more of a particular stock as its price rises? My advice is: don't! You'll only minimize your gains. Let's see how this works. Suppose you buy 500 shares of stock Z at $6 per share. The price then goes up to $7/share, you're encouraged by the prospects and decide to buy 500 more shares at that price. Your total investment is:

500 shares @ $6/share	$3,000	
500 shares @ $7/share	3,500	
Total cost	$6,500	

You're still making $500 on your original investment (less commissions) since your stock is now worth $7,000 and cost only $6,500. This, however, represents only a 7.7 percent return on your investment. If you had not purchased the additional shares, your return would still have been $500, but it would represent an appreciation of 16.7 percent. It's easy to see that the more you average upward, the more your rate of return is decreased on your original investment.

Suppose the stock goes up to $8/share. You're even

more enthusiastic about it so you decide to buy 500 more shares. Your investment now is:

500 shares @ $6/share	$ 3,000
500 shares @ $7/share	3,500
500 shares @ $8/share	4,000
Total	$10,500

Let's say the stock stays @ $8/share for months and months, so you decide to sell at that price. Your 1500 shares will bring in $12,000, or a $1,500 profit (14.3 percent) on your original investment of $10,500. If you had not purchased the last 500 shares, your profit would still be $1,500 on your original $6,500 investment, but at a rate of return of 23 percent. However, if you had never averaged up at all, your profit on your original shares would have been $1,000 (500 shares at $8/share equals $4,000 minus the original $3,000 purchase price). This represents a rate of return of 33⅓ percent.

The situation really becomes disastrous if the stock goes down after you have averaged upward. Suppose, after purchasing the 1,500 shares, the stock returns to its original $6/share and stays there. You decide to sell, bringing you $9,000. This represents a $1,500 loss at a rate of 14.3 percent. If you had not averaged upward, your loss would have been zero (minus commissions).

The advice still holds: Average downward on good stocks, but never upward, no matter how good you think they are. Try to purchase what you want when they are low. If they move up, just sit back and wait to take your profits after the advance is over. (You can put stop orders or orders to sell slightly below the stock's price, in order to protect profits you already have.) Your rate of return increases dramatically in proportion to how far the stock price moves upward.

7

WHEN TO SELL

Your primary guide of when to sell an individual stock is the action and performance of the stock itself as it reacts to the changing financial picture of the company it represents, to market trends, and to the financial state of the economy.

RISING STOCK PRICES, BULL MARKET

Let us begin with an ideal situation: your stock is moving steadily upward in response to increases in company earnings, net profits, and earnings per share, during a bull market and during a rapidly improving national economy. Unless you absolutely need the money, you'd be very foolish to sell under these circumstances. As long as these trends continue, hold on, ride it out, and enjoy the maximum profit possible after the upward-trend is over.

LEVEL STOCK PRICE

Any one of a number of factors may interrupt this joy ride. The most important factor occurs when the price of the stock levels off. I don't mean for just one day or even a week or so, but for several weeks. This could mean nothing, or it could mean something important. Your job is to find out what it means. Is the stock still selling at a reasonable P/E ratio?

(Reasonable would be defined here as no greater than the average for the market.) When the P/E ratio of the whole market averages 8 (as it did during the 1982 recession), I began to consider selling stocks that had stopped advancing in price and had reached the average ratio. When the market averages 13 (as it did during the middle of 1983) and a stock had stopped advancing, I would usually try to sell it after the P/E ratio had reached that figure. As long as the stock price continued to advance, however, even well beyond the average P/E ratio, there is no point in selling it. I would keep putting stop orders at higher and higher figures, however, to protect the profits I had already made.

If the stock is *still* selling at a reasonable ratio, the next step is to find out what the corporation is doing. Look especially at earnings first. Have earnings begun to decline? What are the projections for the coming quarter, or year? Declining earnings is one of the major causes of a leveling off or decline in the price of the stock. Also look at the other considerations I've discussed in Chapter 3: annual sales and profit figures of the corporation, coupled with projections of these figures, the financial health of the company, the prospects for the industry, special facts about the company that might be influencing the price of the stock, and opinions about the stock in the investment community.

Any one of a number of factors may influence the stock profits: if sales, profits, or profit margins are falling, the company is facing bad times ahead, if the prospects for the industry are waning, if the company has started to borrow heavily or excessively, if current assets in relation to current liabilities have fallen dangerously low, or if major analysts or stockbrokers have issued a sell notice on the stock. This last fact alone may cause a pause or decline in the advance of the price of any stock.

If, after investigation, your stock comes out smelling

like a rose when all the criteria for selecting a particular company have been applied to your company, you certainly can't say that you need to sell it because of the internal happenings of the company. It may be that the upward pause is temporary while many investors reap their profits. The stock will take off again after the selling is over and other investors discover what a good buy it still is. As suggested previously, I would put a stop order (an order to sell) at a price somewhat lower than the actual price of the stock, in order to protect profits already made.

Of course, the P/E ratio, earnings reports, and other financial data on the company may still be favorable. But, if, in looking ahead, analysts are seeing a decline in sales or a sharp falling off of business in that particular industry, I'd sell immediately.

BEAR MARKET

The hard question is: What do you do when the market gets bearish in anticipation of a stagnant or declining economy? As long as your individual stock is still going up and the financial picture of the individual company is a good one, I'd hold onto the stock, at least for a while, even though the rest of the market is going down. The strongest stocks may continue to increase some, contrary to the market and the economy. They won't go up as much or for as long as they would in a bull market, but they may advance nevertheless. You can't tell what your stock is going to do unless you hold on to it and see. Here again, though, I'd place a stop order to protect profits already made.

Once your stock has peaked and begins to decline, I'd unload it immediately. It's important to remember that the best time to sell is after a stock has peaked and begun to decline, not while it is still on the rise. You may miss the exact high, but if you always sell while your stocks are on the rise, chances are you'll miss out on substantial profits. The mistake many investors make is to take good profits while the stock is still undervalued and on the rise. If they would wait awhile longer, the best profits may yet come. Note: this applies only if the stock is undervalued and still increasing in price.

FALLING STOCK PRICE, BEAR MARKET

Let us now consider the complete opposite of an ideal situation: Your stock is falling in response to adverse financial reports of the company, and the whole market has turned bearish in anticipation of a stagnating or declining economy. What do you do? Sell immediately, even at a loss. With all of these factors working against you, chances are your stock will continue to decline in price, and you'll lose even more money if you hold onto it. It's better to sell now and lose some, then to hold on and lose a lot. Besides, you'll have cash to invest in other stocks after the market has hit bottom. If you hold on, you may not have any money to buy when you should: after the recession has bottomed out.

STEADY OR RISING PRICE, BEAR MARKET

Suppose the whole stock market has turned bearish, but your stock is still remaining fairly steady or increasing slightly. It is still selling at a low P/E ratio, company sales, profits, and earnings are bright, and the company is not likely to be affected adversely by a coming recession. What would you do? I'd hold on, at least for awhile. The real question is: After a thorough investigation of the stock and its company, would you buy into it now at the price asked if you did not already own it? If the answer is yes, then there is certainly no reason to sell what you already hold. A good stock is a good stock, and there is no point in selling what you'd like to own. You have to remember, though, that it takes an especially strong stock to rise during a bear market that is anticipating a sluggish economy. Most stocks follow the trends of the market, no matter how strong they are. If it's really good, hold on to it, as long as it's steady or increasing in price. If it's only average or below, and it starts to decline, sell it.

FALLING STOCK PRICE, BULL MARKET

The opposite situation is where your stock starts falling in the midst of a bull market. Obviously, something is wrong, and you need to find out fast. Make a thorough investigation first of the company whose stock you hold. Many times, such an investigation reveals that the stock has been overbought and is selling at a higher price than financial data would indicate is warranted, and so a correction is underway. Or possibly, you discover financial or internal problems in the company that are affecting the price of the stock. If the stock has been overbought and has too high a P/E ratio, I'd sell it immediately once it has peaked and started to decline in price. If the company is having financial or internal problems, are these temporary or long-lasting? If it is the latter and is not subject to quick correction and adjustment, I'd sell immediately. If the problem is of a temporary nature (a bad earnings report for the latest quarter, but a bright picture ahead, for example), I'd hold on. If I had profits, I'd put a stop order to protect them, just in case the decline continued.

If you don't find any 'financial or internal problems in the company, then get as much information as you can about the future prospects for the industry the company is a part of. It may be that analysts are already seeing trouble way down the road for the industry: six months from now, sales will fall way off. As a result, the stocks representing companies in that industry start taking a nose dive, even though the stock market and the economy are on the rise. This happened recently with the video games industry. At the very time that profits were at a peak, analysts were already looking ahead, seeing a saturated market and declining sales. Once these facts were disclosed, every company in the industry took a major nose dive. If this starts to happen, get out fast.

Essentially, I'd apply the same ten (but opposite) considerations in determining when and which stocks to sell that I apply in determining which stocks to buy (See Chapter 3). If a particular stock is a good buy at a particular time, it's also a good one to hold on to. If it is a bad buy at a particular time, it's a bad one to hold on to and ought to be sold.

8

PYRAMIDING

MEANING AND METHOD

Pyramiding is starting out with a few shares of stock and gradually adding to that number until you own hundreds or thousands. One way to do it is to keep investing more and more of your money in the market so that the value of your holdings will multiply over the years. I've suggested in Chapter 5, however, that you should not buy during those periods when the market is at a peak or on a downtrend. Save your money during those times and wait to invest it after the market is depressed and/or bottoming out. This way you can pick up more shares at bargain prices.

Adding to holdings by using only out-of-pocket money, however, is a slow way to get rich, unless you have such a large income that you always have plenty of money left over at the end of the month to invest. Most investors are not that fortunate.

A better way to pyramid holdings is to keep buying more shares than you sell. How do you do this? By continually buying stocks that are much cheaper in price than the ones you sell. Of course, as I've cautioned, don't buy stocks just because they are cheap. Buy stocks that are selling for $10 per share or less, but buy only on the basis of their fundamental value.

Examples: Let us suppose you bought 500 shares of a stock a year ago at $6 per share. It has increased in value rapidly and is now selling at $14 per share, some 14 times earnings (earnings are $1 per share). The price seems to have peaked and will probably remain fairly steady, oscillating around that price during the coming six months. Company earnings also seem to have leveled off. The market remains bullish. The present time seems like a good opportunity to unload and to buy something else. So you sell your 500 shares @ $14 per share and pocket your $7,000 (commissions will not be included here in our calculations).

Investigation reveals an exceptionally good buy @ $4 per share and another one at $6 per share. You then take your $7,000 and buy 1000 shares of the $4 stock and 500 shares of the $6 one. The important point is that by buying two stocks at prices considerably lower than the price of the one you are selling, you have been able to increase your holdings from 500 to 1500 shares and have diversified as well. Please remember, however, that you never buy a stock just because it's cheap. You buy it because it is a good buy and a sound value at the price offered.

If you have made good selections and the market remains fairly strong, your two stocks should increase in value. Let's say you hit it right on both of them. Your $4 stock increases in value to 12½ per share before you feel that it has reached its peak. You sell it when it has tapered off to $12. Your $6 stock goes up to $10 before you determine you'd better sell it. So you collect $12,000 ($12 × 1000 shares) from one stock and $5,000 ($10 × 500) from the other one. You now have $17,000 to invest—which you do—in stocks selling for $3, $4, $4½, and $5½ per share. You buy 1,000 shares of each—4,000 shares totalling $17,000. Note the leverage that you have achieved. If your stocks go up an average of one point each, you make $4,000 (less commissions), which is a 23.5 percent profit on your $17,000. Additional movement upward will add to your profit and the percent value on your investment. Remember that you started out with only 500 shares at $6 per share. A movement upward of one point at that time would have given you only $500 profit, a 16.7 percent return on your investment. The total return has increased, and the rate of return has also gone up because you have been buying cheaper stocks than the ones you sold.

If you can keep doing this, selling as high as possible and buying more and more shares at considerably cheaper prices, you can multiply the number of shares you own until a very slight movement upward gives you a big profit. How would you like to own 10,000 or more shares? One point up and you make $10,000 or more. This is not an impossible figure if you continue to pyramid your holdings by buying low-priced stocks.

WHEN YOU HIT IT BIG

Of course, once in awhile you'll hit it big. You'll have a stock that really takes off and makes you a lot of money. Let it be! DON'T sell it just because you bought it at $5 and it's now $20, as long as it keeps going up and is still a good buy at the higher prices. DO place a stop order slightly below its price, however, to protect your profits. (See Chapter 7 for details.) With the money you make from one or two such stocks, you can often buy several thousand shares of a much lower-priced stock. But here again, don't sell just because one is high, and don't buy simply because another is low. Buy on the basis of sound value, and don't put your desire to own more shares ahead of your good judgment about the worth of a stock.

There are investors that buy penny stocks—really cheap ones selling for a dollar or so less per share—simply because they are cheap, and because they can own thousands of shares. They have terrific leverage and can make a lot of money if their stocks appreciate. But if the stocks are not good, they can also lose a lot of money—and fast.

WHEN YOU MAKE
A BAD CHOICE

Of course, once in awhile you'll make a bad choice, or your timing will be bad. Your stock will go down because of disappointing financial statements from the company, because it was too high-priced when you bought it, or because the whole market is bearish and carries your stock down along with it. (See Chapter 7 in making decisions about selling.) Even under such circumstances if you have to sell at a loss and if you can buy more shares of an even cheaper, but better stock, you may be able to recoup your losses very easily.

Suppose you bought 1,000 shares of a stock at $9 per share, and it goes down to $7 per share and stays there, with little possibility of improvement in the next year. You sell, collecting $7,000, but find a wonderful stock at $3.50 per share. You decide to buy 2,000 shares of this stock. Now, this stock has only to go up one point before you make up your $2,000 loss on the previous stock. Beyond that, it's all profit.

BROADENING
YOUR PORTFOLIO

There is another important reason for owning a lot of shares: you can broaden your portfolio. Instead of having all your money in one or two companies, you can own stock in a number of different ones. This dilutes your risk by spreading your investments among different firms. If one of these investments is a disappointing one you can make up for it from the earnings of your other investments. I don't think anyone can tell you how much money to invest in any one company. It all depends upon the total amount you have invested. When you first start investing and are able to buy only a limited number of shares, you may have to start with only one or two companies. But as you earn more money, keep broadening your base by investing in additional firms. However, I don't like to have too many different ones. It's too hard to watch them all at once, but neither do I like to put all my eggs in one basket. There is a need to diversify—industries as well as companies.

BUYING
A HIGHER PRICE STOCK

Once in awhile, you may want to buy a stock at a price higher than one you sell. Don't carry this to an extreme. If you sell 1,000 shares of a $5 stock to buy 500 shares of a $10 stock, you're minimizing your chances of greater earnings, unless the $10 stock is really that much better than the $5 one. If the $10 stock moves up one point, it's a 10 percent increase, bringing you a $500 profit. But if the $5 stock moves up one point, it's a 20 percent increase bringing you $1,000 profit. It may be that the $10 stock will move up very far and fast, simply because it is such a good buy. If so, it's certainly preferred over the cheaper stock.

I have known buyers who have sold 1,000 shares of a good $5 stock to buy 200 shares of a good $25 stock. Most of the time, this just doesn't pay off. The $25 stock will have to move up five points for each one point movement of the $5 stock in order to earn the same profit. I know that the percent increase of both is the same—20 percent—but the probabilities of an equal increase are not the same, even if both stocks —in relation to one another—are equally good buys.

9

BUYING
ON MARGIN

MEANING

Buying a stock on margin means that you pay for only a portion of the cost of the stock, borrowing the rest of the money from your brokerage firm. The federal government, through the Board of Governors of the Federal Reserve System (FRB), sets the margin rate, which as of Jan. 3, 1974, is at 50 percent. In other words, you must pay half the cost of the stock. The other half may be financed.

RATES AND RULES

The margin rate has varied over the years. Table 9.1 shows how initial margin requirements have changed in line with the FRB's decision to reduce or increase the amount of credit available for margining securities. Changes in initial requirements (the percentage you have to pay when you buy the stock) are not retroactive, meaning that you do not have to deposit additional money if the FRB later raises the initial margin requirement above the rate you've already used. However, your loan value on the stock drops to the current prevailing rate, which will affect your subsequent margin trades. If the market value of your stock increases, you can usually withdraw a percentage of the increase to buy additional stock, subject to the restrictions of your broker.

TABLE 9.1
Initial Margin Requirements

DATES	PERCENT MARGINED
Oct. 29, 1929	No government regulated margin
Oct. 15, 1934 to Jan. 31, 1936	45%
Feb. 1, 1936 to Oct. 31, 1937	55%
Nov. 1, 1937 to Feb. 4, 1945	40%
Feb. 5, 1945 to July 4, 1945	50%
July 5, 1945 to Jan. 20, 1946	75%
Jan. 21, 1946 to Jan. 31, 1947	100%
Feb. 1, 1947 to Mar. 29, 1949	75%
March 30, 1949 to Jan. 16, 1951	50%
Jan. 17, 1951 to Feb. 19, 1953	75%
Feb. 20, 1953 to Jan. 3, 1955	50%
Jan. 4, 1955 to Apr. 22, 1955	60%
Apr. 23, 1955 to Jan. 15, 1958	70%
Jan. 16, 1958 to Aug. 4, 1958	50%
Aug. 5, 1958 to Oct. 15, 1958	70%
Oct. 16, 1958 to July 27, 1960	90%
July 28, 1960 to July 9, 1962	70%
July 10, 1962 to Nov. 5, 1963	50%
Nov. 6, 1963 to June 7, 1968	70%
June 8, 1968 to May 5, 1970	80%
May 6, 1970 to Dec. 5, 1971	65%
Dec. 6, 1971 to Nov. 23, 1972	55%
Nov. 24, 1972 to Jan. 2, 1974	65%
Jan. 3, 1974 to _____	50%

There is another initial requirement that must be met. It is called the New York Stock Exchange minimum initial requirement. Under this requirement, you must establish an equity equal to at least $2,000 every time you enter into a new commitment in your general margin account.

When a stock drops in price below the purchase cost, all firms have a minimum equity that they require in order to maintain the account. The NYSE rule is 25 percent. This means you must maintain an equity in your margin account of at least 25 percent of the current market value of a NYSE common stock purchased on margin. If your total goes below this, you have to add additional equity to your account. If you cannot, the firm has a right to sell your security to get their money. Most firms have an even more stringent requirement. A 30 percent equity requirement is quite common.

ADVANTAGES

The big advantage of buying on margin is that you increase your leverage: you stand to make a much greater profit (or to lose a greater amount) with less money. Let's see how this works. Suppose you buy 1,000 shares of a $5 stock. You buy on margin, paying $2,500 and borrow the rest. The stock goes up to $8 per share and you sell. Your profit is $3,000 (less commissions and interest on the borrowed money). This means you have made $3,000 by paying only $2,500. This represents a 120 percent return on your investment. What would this actually amount to taking into account commission rates and interest paid? Here we have to make some reasonable assumptions. Let's suppose you've purchased your stock from a discount brokerage house and pay a 1.4 percent commission to buy (amounting to $70) and a 1.4 percent to sell (amounting to $112), for a total of $182. Let's further suppose that the interest charged you is at an annual rate of 12 percent, and you've kept the stock for one year before selling, so you pay 12 percent on the $2,500 borrowed, or $300. Your total costs are $182 commissions and $300 interest, or $482. This, subtracted from your profit of $3,000, gives you a net profit of $2,518. This still represents 101 percent return on your $2,500.

Now let's see what profit you would have made if you had paid for the stock in full, amounting to a total of $5,000. Your gain is the same, $3,000. Commissions are still $182. Interest is zero. Your net profit would be $3,000 minus $182 equals $2,818. But this is the return on $5,000 invested (not $2,500, as when you purchased on margin). In this case, your return is 56 percent: still a handsome profit, but certainly not as good as the 101 percent from buying on margin.

It's quite evident that buying on margin multiplies your chances of profits, but it also enables you to diversify your investment. If instead of purchasing 1,000 shares of stock in one company at $5 per share, you buy 2,000 shares of stock on margin—1,000 from each of two companies at $5 per share—you're diluting your risk through diversification. So if you lose on one stock, you still have a chance of gaining on the other.

Thus, let's suppose that you purchased 1,000 shares of one stock that went up from $5 to $8. You also purchased 1,000 shares of another one at $5 per share, and it subsequently went down to $3 per share. You're forced to sell it after one year. How do you come out? Your profit on the first is $2,518. The losses on the second stock are:

Decline in price		$2,000
Commissions		
1.4% to buy	$70	
2.0% to sell	60	130
Interest		
12% × $2,500	—	300
Total		$2,430

Your total profit is still $88 ($2,518 minus $2,430). Of course, if one stock goes down as much or more than the other one gains, you'll still lose, but you certainly won't lose as much as if you had put all your money in the losing stock.

RISKS AND REGULATIONS

The real catch, of course, is that when you buy on margin, and a stock goes down, you will lose greater percentages of your money than if you had paid cash. Leverage works both ways. It multiplies your profits when you win, and it multiplies your losses when you lose. Thus, on the stock already discussed, if you bought 1,000 shares @ $5 per share, on 50 percent margin, paying $2,500 and it goes down to $3 per share, and you're forced to sell after one year, your losses would be:

Price decline	$2,000
Commissions	130
Interest	300
Total	$2,430

This represents a 97.2 percent loss on your total investment of $2,500! You're almost wiped out! Of course, if you had paid cash for the stock, you'd have lost almost as much total money, $2,130 ($2,000 plus $130 commissions), but this would have represented only 42.6 percent of your total investment. The possibility of greater percentage losses when buying on margin, as well as the possibility of greater profits, ought to make you especially careful to buy only the very best stocks at times when they are most likely to appreciate in value and not go down. If, after buying on margin, your stock goes down below the minimum maintenance percentage that has been established, your broker has a right to ask for additional collateral to cover your losses. If you don't have it, and are forced to sell to repay your loan, you're perhaps stuck with greater losses than you would ordinarily have suffered.

The possibility of loss has resulted in strict regulations and requirements that govern margin trading. As mentioned, the FRB requires a 50 percent margin, but individual houses may tighten the requirement. One nationwide brokerage house requires a 70 percent margin (meaning you have to pay 70 percent of the cost of the stock). The federal government also decides which stocks are marginable. All NYSE and American and some Regional Exchanges stocks can be purchased on margin. But only a limited selection of OTC stocks can be. Your broker can send you such a list. Here again, individual brokers may not liberalize the federal regulations, but they can make them more stringent. For example, many brokers will not margin a stock selling for $3 per share or less (there's too great a chance of your being wiped out if it declines in price). Other brokers limit marginable stocks to those selling above a certain price.

There's no law which says a broker has to sell you stocks on margin. If a firm thinks you've made a poor investment or you're a poor credit risk, they can refuse to give you a margin account. Some brokers require an initial cash deposit to open a margin account that is above the $2,000 required by the NYSE—$3,000 to $5,000 is not unusual. Of course, you may purchase stock from this account, but the initial deposit is required. Some insist on a minimum amount of collateral (for example: $3,000) in your account at all times to keep the account open.

INTEREST RATES

What interest rate is charged to you on money loaned to you? All brokers calculate this on the basis of what they call the *broker call loan rate*. This is the rate at which a brokerage firm can borrow money. The interest rate charged to you is always figured at a certain percentage above the broker call loan rate. Thus, brokers can borrow money at one figure, loan it to you at a greater figure, and make money by loaning you money. Some houses will even loan you cash advances or offer you a Visa card to make purchases with.

Some houses charge you a 'fixed rate of interest above the broker's call rate—for example, one percent on margin accounts—regardless of the size of your account. Other houses have a scale of interest charges, with the rate decreasing as the size of the account grows. One house, for example, charges interest on the following scale:

AMOUNT OWED	INTEREST CHARGED ABOVE BROKER'S CALL RATE
$0–$ 9,999	2%
$10,000–$24,999	1½%
$25,000–$49,999	1%
$50,000–$99,999	½%
$100,000 and over	¼%

As with anything else, the larger your account, the cheaper you are able to get money.

SHOPPING AROUND

Before you buy on margin, you need to shop around to find out what the margin requirements, rules, and rates are as established by each firm. Discount houses offer margin accounts along with the full-service firms. All firms require an account application that includes a disclosure of your financial situation and a check on your credit rating. If you have good credit and are a regular customer with a firm that knows you, you shouldn't have any trouble opening a margin account. If they don't know you, they'll check on you and see if you're eligible. If you're new to the market, my advice to you is to trade modestly on a cash-only basis until you know what you're doing. You can then expand your operations, including opening margin accounts, after you are more experienced.

10

COMMISSIONS

REGULATED COMMISSIONS

Up until May 1, 1975, the minimum commissions that members of the various stock exchanges were permitted to charge were set by the S.E.C. Table 10.1 shows those rates in round lots of 100, 200, 500, and 1,000 shares of stocks selling for $1 to $10 per share. I have given the rates in terms of the percentage commission one would have to pay for each $1 invested. Figures are rounded out to the nearest tenth of a percent.

TABLE 10.1
Regulated Commissions Fees, Prior to May 1, 1975

| PRICE/SHARE | NUMBER OF SHARES | | | |
| | 100 | 200 | 500 | 1000 |
		Rate per $1 Invested		
1	9.2%	9.2%	9.2%	9.2%
2	5.7	5.7	5.7	5.4
3	4.6	4.6	4.5	4.0
4	4.0	4.0	3.7	3.3
5	3.6	3.6	3.3	2.8
6	3.4	3.4	2.9	2.8
7	3.2	3.2	2.6	2.6
8	3.1	3.1	2.4	2.4
9	2.9	2.9	2.3	2.3
10	2.8	2.8	2.1	2.1

Actually, according to this schedule, you saved money by buying the most expensive stocks ($10/share) rather than by buying the cheapest ones ($1/share). And there was no difference in commission rates on lots less than 500 shares. Once you started buying in 500 or 1,000 share lots, however, you could save money. Thus, to buy and sell 1,000 shares of an $8 stock would have cost you a minimum of 4.8 percent (2.4 percent x 2). Any earnings above that figure were profit. However, buying and selling a stock for $1 per share would have cost you 18.4 percent (9.2 percent x 2). Your stock would have had to appreciate well above this figure before you could have made any profit.

FULL-SERVICE COMMISSIONS

Remembering that commissions were deregulated and brokerage firms can set any fee they want, how do these rates compare with those of the major full-service houses today? Today's rates are higher, as one might expect, due partly to inflation and the higher cost of doing business.

Table 10.2 shows today's rates in terms of a percentage of each $1 spent on stocks (selling for $1 to $10/share) in round lots of 100, 200, 500, and 1,000 shares. The rates are actual quotes from 6/1/83 of four major full-service firms: Merrill, Lynch, Pierce, Fenner, and Smith (column 1); E. P. Hutton (column 2); Paine-Webber (column 3); and Kidder-Peabody (column 4). Percentages are rounded to the nearest one-tenth percent. These quotes are subject to change at any time. All firms are willing to negotiate rates with their best, large-volume customers. But these are the quotes I received over the phone from local brokerage houses. The actual rates

TABLE 10.2
Commission Rates of Four Full-Service Brokerage Firms, June 1, 1983

NUMBER OF SHARES

PRICE/SHARE	100 Rate/$1 Invested				200 Rate/$1 Invested				500 Rate/$1 Invested				1,000 Rate/$1 Invested			
	1	2	3	4	1	2	3	4	1	2	3	4	1	2	3	4
1	10%	15%	10%	16.2%	10%	15%	10%	14.1%	10%	14%	10%	13.2%	10%	12.2%	10%	11.5%
2	10	9.5	9.6	9.4	9.5	9.5	9.4	8.4	9.6	8	7.7	7.9	7.1	7.1	7.2	6.7
3	10	6.3	7.1	7.1	5.5	6.3	6.9	6.4	5.9	6	5.8	6.1	5.2	5.3	5.3	5.0
4	7.5	5.5	5.9	6.1	5.3	5.5	5.7	5.5	4.9	5	4.9	5.0	4.3	4.4	4.3	4.1
5	6.0	5.0	5.1	5.3	4.8	5.0	5.0	4.9	4.2	4.4	4.3	4.3	3.6	3.7	3.7	3.5
6	5.0	4.7	4.6	4.9	4.4	4.7	4.5	4.5	3.8	3.8	3.8	3.8	3.4	3.3	3.3	3.3
7	4.3	4.3	4.2	4.6	4.1	4.3	4.2	4.2	3.4	3.4	3.4	3.4	3.1	3.0	3.0	3.0
8	3.8	4.1	4.0	4.3	3.9	4.0	3.9	4.0	3.1	3.3	3.2	3.2	2.8	2.8	2.8	2.8
9	3.9	3.8	3.8	4.0	3.7	3.8	3.7	3.8	2.9	3.0	3.0	2.9	2.7	2.6	2.6	2.6
10	3.5	3.6	3.6	3.8	3.5	3.6	3.6	3.6	2.7	2.8	2.8	2.8	2.5	2.5	2.5	2.4

Column 1: Merrill, Lynch, Pierce, Fenner, and Smith
Column 2: E. F. Hutton
Column 3: Paine-Webber
Column 4: Kidder-Peabody & Co.

you are charged in your area may be different. Most firms have a minimum fee for any transaction.

It is quite obvious that the rates in all of the columns are very similar to one another. Some are a little higher at one point and a little lower at another, but they remain quite competitive with one another throughout the gamut.

SAVING ON COMMISSIONS

It is also obvious that by scrutinizing the chart carefully, you can cut your commission rates considerably when you do buy. The highest rate is 16.2 percent. The lowest is 2.4 percent. This is quite a difference. If you double these figures, your stock will cost you from 32.4 percent to 4.8 percent to be bought and sold. As far as I'm concerned, the upper figures that are charged for stocks selling at $1/share are prohibitive. The higher priced the stock is and the more shares you buy, the lower the commission rate. If you buy 500 shares of a $3 stock, you'll pay a commission of around 6 percent. Double the figure (12 percent) is what you'll pay to buy and sell it. If you buy 1,000 shares of the $3 stock, your commission rate drops to around 5 percent (10 percent to both buy and sell). Thus, you'd pay 10 percent times $3,000 or $300 in commissions. If, however, you buy 1,000 shares of a $9 stock, your rate is about 2.6 percent (5.2 percent to buy and sell). You do pay a penalty for buying the cheapest stock, but you can buy more shares, so the overall amount is not too different. Thus, if you have $5,000 to spend, you could buy 500 shares of a $10 stock, paying a commission rate of around 2.8 percent (5.6 percent to buy and sell), or you could buy 1,000 shares of a $5 stock, paying a commission rate of around 3.6 percent (7.2 percent to buy and sell). The total difference in cost to buy and sell amounts to: $80. This really is not significant enough to worry about on a $5,000 investment. The important consideration is which stock is the better buy? If the $5 stock is, buying it will more than make up for the difference in commission between it and the $10 stock. It is quite obvious though that it is to your distinct advantage to try to trade in 500 and 1,000 share lots. You'll save a lot on commissions.

DISCOUNT BROKERAGE FIRMS

Another way to save on commissions is to buy and sell through discount brokerage houses. Discount brokers charge considerably lower commissions than do the large, full-service firms already discussed. They are able to save you money because they don't do investment research, and they don't employ commissioned salespeople to give you investment advice. However, if you select your own stocks, as this book should enable you to do, all you need is a firm to make speedy, efficient transactions for you. The discount houses do this very nicely.

Despite considerable savings on commissions, an overwhelming number of investors will deal only with a full-service broker. One survey indicated that 83 percent of active investors use only such brokers (Dan Dorfman, "Schwab Rate No. 1," San Francisco *Examiner,* Sept. 23, 1982). Seventy-eight percent of very active, substantial buyers do the same. By the same token, between 5 and 6 percent of 1,000 investors indicated that they used only discount brokers. Apparently, broker loyalty runs very high. Investors like the person-to-person relationship. Active investors averaged 1.6 brokers; substantial investors, 1.9 (Dorfman, 1982).

The following is a partial list of some of the discount houses in the United States, together with their toll-free numbers. (If you live in a state where a specific firm is located, you may not be able to call it on the number given. You will

probably have to get the special in-state number for it from
your operator.) Most of the firms have offices in New York.
Some have additional offices across the country. The firms
are listed alphabetically. The list doesn't pretend to be complete. There are about 100 discount firms in the United States
alone. Some of these would be only in your locale, but the list
should help you get a lot of information. I would call them and
ask them to send you their brochures and commission rates.

DISCOUNT BROKERAGE FIRMS

Firm/Telephone Number	*State or City*
Andrew Peck Associates 1–800–221–5873	New York
Brown and Co. 1–800–225–6767	Boston; Florida
Carnegie Discount Brokerage 1–800–223–1988	New York; Los Angeles; Chicago
Charles Schwab & Co., Inc. 1–800–228–6603	49 offices across the U.S.
Chemical Investor Services 1–800–223–5556	New York (Chemical Bank)
Fidelity/Source 1–800–225–2097	Boston; New York; New Jersey; many local offices
First Heritage Capital Co. 1–800–621–7011	New York; Chicago; San Francisco
Icahn and Co., Inc. 1–800–223–2188	New York
Kenneth Kass & Co., Inc. 1–800–526–4472	New Jersey; Connecticut; New York
Marsh Block & Co., Inc. 1–800–221–2255	New York
Muriel Siebert 1–800–821–8200	New York

Pacific Brokerage Services	New York; California
1–800–223–3242	
Rose & Co.	Los Angeles; New York;
1–800–621–3700	Philadelphia; Pittsburgh;
	San Francisco; Washington,
	D.C.; Boston; Chicago;
	Houston
Seaport Securities	New York; Boston
1–800–221–9894	
Stock Cross	Boston
1–800–225–6196	
Tradex Brokerage Service, Inc.	New York; Houston
1–800–221–7874	
Waterhouse Securities, Inc.	New York; San Francisco;
1–800–421–9563	Los Angeles
Werlitz Securities, Inc.	New York
1–800–221–7795	

DISCOUNT RATES

How much can you save by going through discount houses? This depends on the firm, but savings range from 40 to 75 percent, based upon the total amount of the transaction. Table 10.3 shows the commission rates of four different discount houses. The rates given are the percentages charged per $1 invested on stocks selling in lots of 500 or 1,000 shares and selling for $1 to $10 per share. These rates are subject to change at any time. Some houses charge lower rates, but the figures given here will enable you to compare rates with full-service houses and rates from houses that are even cheaper. Your best bet is to call several different houses and make the comparisons yourself.

TABLE 10.3
Commission Rates * of Four Different Discount
Brokerage Houses, June 1, 1983

PRICE/ SHARE	500 SHARES RATE/$1 INVESTED				1,000 SHARES RATE/$1 INVESTED			
	1	2	3	4	1	2	3	4
1	8%	6.4%	8.4%	9.0%	6.4%	3.6%	5.7%	7.0%
2	4%	3.6%	4.2%	4.5%	3.2%	2.2%	2.9%	3.5%
3	2.7	2.7	2.8	3.0	2.1	1.7	1.9	2.3
4	2.1	2.2	2.1	2.3	1.6	1.5	1.4	1.8
5	1.9	1.9	1.8	2.0	1.3	1.4	1.3	1.4
6	1.8	1.7	1.5	1.8	1.2	1.3	1.1	1.2
7	1.6	1.6	1.3	1.6	1.1	1.2	0.9	1.1
8	1.5	1.5	1.2	1.5	1.0	1.2	0.8	1.0
9	1.4	1.4	1.0	1.4	0.9	1.1	0.7	1.0
10	1.3	1.4	1.0	1.3	0.9	1.1	0.8	0.9

* Expressed as percent charged for each $1 invested, with percentages rounded to nearest .1 percent.
Firm #1: Charles Schwab & Co., Inc.
Firm #2: Fidelity/Source (Commission Schedule 1)
Firm #3: First Heritage Capital
Firm #4: Rose and Co.

SELECTING
A DISCOUNT FIRM

There are a number of different factors to take into consideration when selecting a discount brokerage firm. Number one is to look for quick, efficient service. Are orders taken promptly (or do they put you on hold for a long time before taking your order over the phone?), accurately, and executed efficiently? You want a house that will buy your stock as quickly as possible once you have put your order in. Much delay in the execution of an order may cost you money if the stock is on the rise when you buy it. You want your firm to have complete access to all security markets. Do they specialize in stocks from only one exchange, or are they able to serve you well on OTC stocks as well as stocks from the various exchanges? What hours are they open to take orders? One house provides 24-hour-a-day, seven-day-a-week service. Of course, orders can be executed only when the exchanges are open, but it is a great convenience to be able to place orders after business hours or on weekends.

You want a house that will report promptly to you once an order has been executed. Some houses provide on-the-line service, and can tell you within minutes that your purchase is complete, without your ever having to hang up the phone. This service, however, is usually available on a limited number of primary issues, and not on the type of secondary issues you buy. Some companies will call you back to notify you when they have purchased or sold your stock, at what price, and so forth. All companies mail you a written confirmation of your order, and should do so promptly.

Of course, you want a company whose financial terms are competitive. This not only means favorable discount rates, but also means receiving the maximum interest on credit balances you have in your account. Firms may require a credit balance of $1,000, $2,000, or $2,500 before they start giving you interest on the money in your account. Most firms require a minimum equity of $2,000 to open a margin account. Similarly, you want reasonable interest charges on debit balances and on margin accounts. Ask various firms for interest and margin rates. You'll also save money if the firm credits dividends and interest to your account on payable dates rather than just once a month. Insist on monthly statements of the status of your account, provided you have some equity, regardless of whether you have traded that month or not.

The larger firms have branch offices at various locations around the country. But now that most firms provide a nationwide toll free telephone system to transact business, it's not so important to have an office near you, unless you just like to visit and get acquainted personally.

Select a firm that will provide up-to-date information on your account at any time, just by your calling in. You may need information on credit or debit balances in your account, security positions, recently executed transactions, and so forth. Some firms will not give reports by telephone, but will mail you the latest computer print-out information. Similarly, you need the latest quotes and information on any stocks you are contemplating buying. Even though discount firms do not generate investment research, many will mail out copies of S & P *Stock Reports* and *Stock Guides* or other basic information sheets.

You need complete custody service for your securities. If you trade very often, chances are you won't have the security certificates mailed to you; it's too much trouble to sign and deliver them each time you sell. This means you want to be certain your holdings are safe. According to the *Securities Investor Protection Act of 1970 as Amended Through 1980,* all security brokers and dealers are required by law to be SIPC (Securities Investor Protection Corporation) members. This means that the securities of each customer are insured up to a maximum of $500,000 (with the protection of the cash in your account limited to $100,000). If you ever have more than that in the account of one broker, make sure that firm carries extra insurance to cover your holdings. Some firms insure up to several million dollars worth of securities. The same law applies to discount brokers that applies to full-commission brokers.

If you need investment advice, you won't get it from a discount broker, but, if you want to save money on commissions and get your advice elsewhere, a discount broker may be for you. Buying or selling securities is done in the same manner whether the firm is a discount brokerage or a full-commission house.

11

TAXES

In addition to learning how to make as much profit as possible on the stock market, you'll also have to learn how to save on taxes. You can only maximize your profits by minimizing your taxes. Short-term profits (those on securities held for one year or less) are taxed as ordinary income, so any gain will be reduced by the percentage that you have to pay out as taxes. One goal, therefore, is to keep taxes to a minimum.

LONG-TERM VERSUS SHORT-TERM CAPITAL GAINS

There are a number of ways of keeping taxes down. One familiar way is to do long-term trades, that is, to hold on to your securities for over one year before selling. This way you'll pay capital gain taxes on only the first 40 percent of your profits, at rates that are in accord with the tax laws at the present time. Your actual tax rate on that 40 percent will depend upon your income, but, under the new law, the maximum is only 50 percent, even if you were in the 70 percent tax bracket before. If you're in the 17 percent tax bracket, you pay taxes at this rate (but on only 40 percent of your profit). Thus, the maximum tax you'll ever have to pay on long-term capital gains is 50 percent of 40 percent of your profits, or 20 percent of the total profit. If you're in the 25 percent tax bracket, your tax rate will be 25 percent of 40 percent of your profits, or 10 percent.

Sometimes, you will want to keep a stock for over a year—not just to save on taxes—because it continues to go up and it is too soon to take profits, or because it hasn't gone up at all (it may even have gone down) and you're waiting for it to rise before selling it. Most of the time, however, I would not let tax considerations be the determining factor in when to sell a stock. By holding on to a stock longer than feasible, you may lose all or part of your profit entirely. The important consideration is: How much profit (after taxes) can I make now in comparison to the profit I would make if I sold the stock after holding on to it over a year? Do what's going to net you the most profit—not what's just going to save you taxes.

IRA AND KEOGH PLANS

There are other ways to save on taxes. One way is to put money in an IRA or Keogh plan and then do your trading with money in the plan. You and your spouse can contribute $2,000 per year each to an IRA if you're both employed. If you are employed and your spouse isn't, you can still contribute $2,250 total per year for the both of you. Not only is the money you put in your IRA tax free (it reduces your income by that amount in the year contributed), but any capital gain, interest, or dividends you make on that money while it is in the plan is also tax free. You can buy and sell stocks with that money for years, make thousands of dollars on it, and never have to pay any taxes on the earnings as long as the money is in the plan. Of course, once you draw any out (you can at age 59½ and after without penalty) it's added to your income that year and taxed as ordinary income at whatever rate applies to your

total income. The only requirement for opening a standard
IRA is that you have had some income earned from a job
during that year. Income from interest or dividends doesn't
qualify.

Keogh plans are for people who get income from self-
employment. That includes those who have a salaried job and
are self-employed on the side. You can put a full 15 percent of
your self-employment income in a Keogh plan per year, up to
a maximum contribution of $15,000, and deduct it from your
taxable income. In 1984 you'll be able to invest as much as 20
percent of your earnings, up to a maximum of $30,000.

There's nothing to prevent a self-employed person from
opening both an IRA and a Keogh account. You can use all of
that money to invest in stocks, if you so desire, and never have
to pay any taxes on capital gains, interest, or dividends earned
as long as you leave the money in your retirement account. Of
course, once you take any of the money out, it's taxed as
ordinary income. If you withdraw any money before age 59½,
you pay a 10 percent penalty fee.

There are those who say it makes no sense to use retirement plans for aggressive investments in growth stocks, when
you can pay a lower long-term capital gains tax if the trading
is done outside the retirement plan. Also, any losses sustained
within an account can't be used to offset other income if the
stocks are in the retirement account. It's true that losses can't
be written off, so using a retirement account becomes a riskier
investment. But the purpose of a retirement account is to build
up equity for your old age, to be taken out at a time when
you won't be paying as much tax. If you can trade wisely, earn
capital gains on each trade, and do this often enough over the
years, the money multiplies very rapidly because it's reinvested
over and over again and because all taxation is deferred over
those years as long as the gains are left in the account. Of

course, you don't have to keep all the money in growth stocks, you can switch some to high interest paying bonds, CD's, or other investments as profits build up. But there is a real advantage to compounding capital gains unhindered by taxes.

THE SHELTERED
RETIREMENT ACCOUNT

There are other ways of avoiding capital gain taxes on stocks. You can set up a tax-sheltered retirement account with an investment firm and do all your trading within this account. Any contributions you make to it are not tax deductible (as in the IRA and Keogh plan), but once the money is in the account, any income or capital gains earned from it is tax deferred until you take the money out. This is similar to a tax-deferred annuity, except that you are permitted to manage your own money in the account.

One such plan is the National Pension Group (NPG) Pension Plan, administered by E. F. Hutton, which allows eligible employees to make after-tax contributions to their NPG tax-sheltered retirement account and earn tax deferred income and capital gains. Once the money is in the plan, investing it is directed by you. You can contribute a maximum of 10 percent of your earnings per year, and 10 percent of prior years' earnings if you have not contributed before. Thus, the provisions can be retroactive to the year you became employed with the firm. You are not obligated to contribute every year, and any unused part of your contribution limit may be carried forward into future years. You may withdraw all or part of the money in your account at any time, but any amount in excess of contributions made that year is taxable as income upon withdrawal. This plan is insured by Securities Investor's Protection Corporation (SIPC) up to $500,000 in securities and $100,000 in cash.

Of course, your employer must join the plan, but it costs him/her nothing. Your employer never contributes a cent to your plan but will only have to supply you with information regarding your earnings. If you change employers, your account stays with you and not your employer.

CLOSELY-HELD CORPORATION

Another way to save on capital gain taxes is to establish your own closely-held corporation. This is often done by physicians, lawyers, and other professional people, and may be done by others who earn money working for themselves. You can establish your own corporation and you and/or other members of your family can retain complete control. Once it is formed, you can pay yourself a salary out of corporate earnings, establish a profit-sharing plan that permits the corporation to contribute up to 15 percent of your income, and start a pension plan that permits an additional corporate contribution of up to 10 percent of your income. The maximum contribution started at $25,000 and has been raised each year. The corporation does not pay taxes on these contributions and the benefits are tax-deferred to the corporate employees who participate in the plan. The funds are held in profit-sharing and pension-plan trusts and may be invested any way, according to the restrictions of the trust agreement. If you are the administrator and trustee of both the pension plan and the profit-sharing trusts, you can make all the investment decisions. Meanwhile, any income and capital gains are tax-deferred. If the corporation suspends operations or is dissolved, you can continue to manage the trust funds if you desire, deferring all corporate taxes and capital gains on the original contribution for years to come. If you decide to have all profit-sharing money and pension money paid to you, it is taxed as ordinary income, but you can income-average the amount for the preceding ten-year period if you were enrolled in the plan for five or more years. Or, you can put all the receipts into another retirement plan, in which case the taxes are deferred. You may withdraw funds from the plans at age 59½ and after without penalty. Special provisions apply to your beneficiaries if you die with any unused funds.

If you're incorporated, you may also set up a voluntary pension plan in addition to the other plans that would permit you to contribute up to 10 percent of your pre-tax earnings. All capital gains, interest, and dividends earned from this plan would be tax-deferred until withdrawn. Any withdrawals made prior to age 59½ are taxed and subject to a 10 percent penalty tax.

My advice to you is to get the help of a tax planner who is an expert on schemes to minimize income taxes and on methods to defer taxes. The more that earnings from your stocks are tax deferred, the more money is left over for additional investments. The compounding effect of being able to earn money on earnings means that your total equity will grow much more than if you were not able to defer taxes.

Let's suppose you save $1,000 the first year on capital gain taxes. If you were able to make 30 percent a year on that money, still tax deferred, at the end of 10 years, you would have saved $10,604.50. If you had invested $10,000 initially, you would have $106,045 saved from not having had to pay capital gain taxes! So you can see, it's very worthwhile to participate in plans that will defer paying capital gain taxes. They allow you to use your pre-tax earnings and to multiply your holdings much more rapidly.

12

SOURCES
OF INFORMATION

A WEALTH OF INFORMATION

One of the things that has always impressed me is the wealth of information available as a guide in selecting stocks. This information is so extensive that there is absolutely no excuse for buying any stock blindly. You can find out everything you need to know before buying a stock in a particular company, even if you have never heard of that company before.

Years ago, my approach to stock buying was to buy stocks in large, well-known companies: IBM, Dupont, Litton, General Motors, Exxon, and so forth. Because such companies were large and familiar, I figured that there was a lot less chance of losing money and a far greater chance of making money in the big companies than if I had invested in smaller, lesser known companies. How wrong I was! I soon discovered that it was quite possible to lose money on stock in any company if you didn't know what you were doing, which I didn't. But I learned, and I learned the hard way (but with very little money invested while I was learning), until gradually I began to be able to sort out facts and figures in a way that made sense and in ways that could be turned into profits.

During this process, I became familiar with the vast stores of information that are available and realized that the answers were there for those who bothered to seek. I began to realize, also, that it didn't take that much time, once you knew where and how to look.

The problem, of course, is that most buyers don't bother. So they end up depending on their brokers and get mad at them when the stocks don't become instant winners. I'm not deprecating the value of good brokers. They can be tremendously helpful. I use their services all the time. But, some are obviously more helpful than others. I've met super ones and terrible ones, but most try their best to help you make money—that's their business.

Most brokers, however, depend on information that is provided by others. The brokers' problem is that they are usually so busy that they don't have time to evaluate the best buys themselves or to sort out the kind of stocks you're looking for. Many are responsible for selling all kinds of stocks, bonds, annuities, retirement accounts, options, futures, and other investments, so they can't possibly become experts in every one of these fields. Even the largest houses, where brokers specialize in certain investments, don't assign any of them, as far as I know, to deal exclusively in low-priced stocks. In fact, many don't like to buy low-priced stocks for you. The investment analysts of these large firms specialize in analyzing stocks by industry groups, not by price, so it becomes very difficult for brokers to sort out the low-priced stocks from voluminous reports.

All of this adds up to the fact that you will have to assume maximum responsibility yourself. There is ample information, readily available and not too difficult to use, once you learn how. All you have to do is vow that you're going to start using it, that you're going to start buying stocks based upon sound facts that you've sorted out yourself, and that you're not going to buy stocks on hunch or hearsay. The purpose of this chapter is to put you in touch with these basic sources of information.

DAILY NEWSPAPERS

You're going to need a good daily newspaper that carries complete price quotations of stocks on the New York Stock Exchange, American Stock Exchange, and Over-the-Counter stocks (NASDAQ). This usually means a fairly large-city newspaper. Many smaller papers carry abbreviated lists, often omitting Over-the-Counter stocks. If your local paper doesn't carry complete quotations, then by all means subscribe to a paper such as the New York *Times* or the *Wall Street Journal*. The *Journal* has built a well-deserved reputation of being the outstanding business and finance daily in the country. And it's available virtually everywhere. It does not come out on Saturday, however, so you'll have to wait until Monday for the results of Friday's trading, if this is the only paper you have access to.

Certainly, the most popular business and financial weekly is *Barron's* which, in addition to including general articles and information, summarizes the results of each week's trading. *Barron's* is especially useful in obtaining interim or fiscal year earnings and up-to-date information on dividends as well as stock prices, weekly sales, yields, P/E ratios, and 50 weeks highs and lows. *Barron's* features an earnings and dividends alert, also. New earnings reports are indicated with an ⟶ besides the stock. Dividend declarations are marked +. Dividend omissions are marked ○

BASIC INFORMATION ON CORPORATIONS

In order to select stocks wisely, you have to be able to get basic factual information on any publicly-held corporation.

Thus, if you are considering buying some stock of a particular company, you need to be able to look the company up to get as much information about it as possible.

The two most important sources of information are published by Standard and Poor and by Moody's *Investor's Service*. Standard and Poor's publications containing basic corporation information include the following:

Stock Guide: the best single source of information on all corporations in the United States in summary form. It is an indispensable publication to have. It is inexpensive, in one small booklet, and is published monthly. Most large brokerage houses will give you a single copy free of charge. Or, you can write Standard and Poor, 345 Hudson Street, N.Y., N.Y. 10014.

S & P Corporation Records: arranged in notebooks with companies on the NYSE, Amex, and NASDAQ in separate volumes. Every broker and most libraries carry these. Look up the companies you're interested in and photostat copies of pages you need. The *yellow section* is the index. The *blue section* contains a list of subsidiary companies and cross references. The *white section* gives descriptions of the different companies and cumulative reports and news on them. There are also daily news and daily cumulative indexes, weekly cumulative indexes, and bi-weekly cumulative indexes to aid you in looking up the very latest information. Thus, quarterly reports of corporations are included along with any special announcements, or recent developments.

S & P Dividend Reports: these are published weekly and summarized in an annual issue.

S & P Earnings Forecaster: published weekly and projects earnings of numerous corporations. Can be quite helpful in appraising the projected earnings of individual corporations.

Moody's *Investor's Service,* 99 Church Street, N.Y., N.Y. 10017, also publishes basic information on corporations. This information is published in seven basic *manuals* as follows:

Industrial Manual
OTC Industrial Manual
Transportation Manual
Public Utility Manual
Bank and Finance Manual
International Manual
Municipal and Government Manual

These manuals are revised three times yearly and are found in most brokerage offices and city libraries. You can photocopy the pages you want on selected corporations.

Moody's also publishes bi-weekly *News Reports* to supplement these manuals. Thus, there are bi-weekly *Industrial News Reports,* bi-weekly *OTC Industrial News Reports,* and so on. Moody's *Complete Corporate Index* is the basic index to the over 20,000 corporations discussed in the manuals. It is revised three times yearly.

Moody's *Investors Fact Sheets:* sheets on individual corporations, similar to the information in the manuals, and as up-to-date as possible.

Moody's *Handbook of Common Stocks:* a bound volume of fact sheets on the most important corporations, published four times yearly: spring, summer, fall, and winter.

You need not lack information on any corporation if you utilize these materials published by Standard and Poor and Moody's.

STOCK BROKERAGE FIRMS

All of the major full-service brokerage firms publish numerous reports, recommendations, letters, and so on to advise their clients on which stocks to buy and to analyze data from different industries and individual corporations. Go to various firms and collect all of the information you can. Ask to be put on their mailing lists. If you buy some stocks from them, they'll keep you on the list and make regular mailings to you. Also, you'll find clippings and coupons in the *Wall Street Journal, Barron's,* and other publications that you can fill out and mail in to receive specific reports. Some of these can be quite helpful. My point of view is that the more information I can receive from more different sources, the better off I am in making selections.

MAGAZINES AND PROFESSIONAL JOURNALS

Don't neglect important articles in magazines that are found on newsstands and in most libraries. Some of the better known magazines include:

Better Investing: Monthly (published out of Michigan)

Business Weekly: Weekly

Financial World: Semi-monthly

Forbes: Semi-monthly

Fortune: Semi-monthly

Money: Monthly

Money Maker: Bi-monthly (published out of Chicago)

Nation's Business: Monthly

The Stock Market Magazine: Monthly

Professional journals include:

Financial Analysts Journal: Bi-monthly

Journal of Finance: Five times a year
The Stockbroker: Quarterly

CHART SERVICES

There are a number of companies that specialize in presenting information in chart form, along with basic statistical financial data. These services go beyond presenting factual data. They give buy and sell recommendations, seeking to guide investors in making wise selections.

Some of the chart services include the following:

Trendline (a S & P Corporation): it publishes information concerning 1476 stocks on NYSE. It also publishes *Daily Action Stock Charts,* weekly, which includes stocks on the NYSE and Amex; and *OTC Chart Manual,* weekly, listing 822 OTC stocks. Most brokerage houses and large libraries carry these.

Value Line Investment Survey: publishes weekly charts and basic information on 1700 stocks.

Daily Graphs: publishes weekly over 1600 stock charts
Harry Lankford: publishes *Quote NY* weekly, which gives 1548 NYSE stock charts, and *Quote American,* which includes 830 Amex stock charts. *Quote OTC* lists 1230 OTC stock charts.

Long Term Values: publishes over 2700 charts monthly on corporations on the NYSE, Amex, and P & F.

My basic criticism of chart services is that many of them chart only the most well-known companies, so that often a company that I want to look up is not included; however, they do a good job on those corporations that are included. If you want to subscribe to chart services, then so be it. See if you can find them at your brokerage house or in the library before subscribing.

INVESTMENT LETTERS
AND ADVISORY SERVICES

What about subscribing to investment advisory services? These services make their money by advising you on what stocks to buy or sell and when. They can be extremely helpful to the buyer who doesn't trust his own judgment completely. I've tried to suggest a procedure by which you can select your own stocks. Once you do choose your own stocks, however, it is a good practice to check with some of the major investment advisory services to see if any of them are recommending any of the stocks you have selected. If they are, it is just one more reason to favor the selections you have made. The mere fact that a major advisory service recommends a stock is often enough to make it spurt up temporarily. If an advisory service issues a sell notice on a stock, try to find out why, and proceed with caution. A sell notice may be enough to make a stock go down.

Of course, you'll find considerable disagreement among the experts. This is why you have to learn to make selections yourself. Just because an advisory service recommends a stock does not mean you should run out and buy it at once. The recommendation may be a different kind of situation than those you like to invest in. You have to make your selections according to the criteria I've selected.

How can you find out what the investment services are recommending? One obvious way is to subscribe to one or more services. Another way is to look up the information in investment digests that summarize what the investment services are recommending. One such publication is called the *Digest of Investment Advice*, published monthly. Another helpful service is the *Hulbert Financial Digest*, also published monthly. Hulbert's publication is unique in that it gives performance ratings of the various investment services themselves, that is, how their stock recommendations actually fared on the market. His summary of how the various advisory services fared for 1982 is given in Table 12.1.

TABLE 12.1
Hulbert's Ratings of Advisory Services for 1982

INVESTMENT LETTERS: A REPORT CARD

Newsletter	1982 Gain	Clarity Rating (a)	No. of Stocks in Portfolio 12/31/82 (b)	Holding Period (Days) (c)
Boswell Report	+57.6%	C	32	201
Cabot Market Letter (Model Portfolio)	+32.8%	A	10	332
Chartist (Long-Term Managed Account)	+23.3%	A	16	151
Dessauer's Journal (Int'l Portfolio)	+18.6%	B	34	1 Yr
The Dines Letter Short-Term Trading Portfolio	− 2.1%	A	0	64
Long-Term Lists: 1. Good Grade Stocks	+16.3%	A	9	84
2. Speculative Stocks	+12.1%	A	8	74

Newsletter	1982 Gain	Clarity Rating (a)	No. of Stocks in Portfolio 12/31/82 (b)	Holding Period (Days) (c)
3. Income Stocks	+20.3%	A	8	68
4. Growth Stocks	+29.4%	A	10	68
5. Precious Metals	− 8.8%	A	11	1 Yr
6. Long-Term Short Sales	+25.4%	A	3	352
Average	+15.8%			
Dow Theory Forecasts				
a. Income Stocks	+12.7%	C	7	1 Yr
b. Investment Stocks	+27.7%	C	10	1 Yr
c. Growth Stocks	+16.7%	C	8	1 Yr
d. Speculative Stocks	+13.3%	C	11	1 Yr
Dow Theory Letters	+20.2%	D	4	?
Dunn & Hargitt Market Guide (20 High Growth) Low P/E Stocks	+ 0.2%	B	20	*
Granville Market Letter	−25.6%	D	30	1 Yr
Green's Commodity Market Comments	+45.8%	A	2	*
Growth Stock Outlook (Supervised Part)	+24.9%	A	27	356
Harry Browne's Special Reports (Variable Portfolio)	+17.2%	A	1	N
Heim Investment Letter (Conservative Portfolio)	− 4.8%	A	0	50
Holt Investment Advisory	− 9.1%	B	27	1 Yr
Howard Ruff's Financial Survival Letter	+33.8%	A	4	?
Int'l Harry Schultz Letter (Investment Table Stocks)	− 0.1%	C	6	188

Newsletter	1982 Gain	Clarity Rating (a)	No. of Stocks in Portfolio 12/31/82 (b)	Holding Period (Days) (c)
Kinsman Advisory Letter	+18.2%	A	8	*
Market Logic				
(Master Portfolio)	+35.8%	B	38	N
Myers Finance & Energy	+12.8%	D	1	?
Outlook (S&P)				
Foundation Stocks	+18.4%	B	2	1 Yr
Growth Stocks	+12.4%	B	6	1 Yr
Speculative Stocks	+30.5%	B	6	1 Yr
Income Stocks	+ 8.4%	B	3	1 Yr
Professional Investor				
NYSE Scan	+39.3%	C	36	78
AMEX Scan	+40.9%	C	32	180
OTC Scan	+23.0%	C	33	138
Investment Grade Stocks	+26.0%	C	7	105
Professional Tape				
Reader (Model P.)	+56.4%	B	36	77
Professional Timing Service				
(Stock Signals)	− 3.4%	C	11	151
RHM Survey	+22.1%	C	45	*
Smart Money	+28.8%	C	19	1 Yr
Speculator	+40.2%	C	58	1 Yr
United Business &				
Investment Services				
Growth Stocks	+16.8%	C	24	1 Yr
Cyclical Stocks	+27.6%	C	14	1 Yr
Income Stocks	+14.7%	C	9	1 Yr
Value Line OTC				
Special Situations	+48.5%	C	12	1 Yr
World Market Perspective	+34.6%	B	2	?
Zweig Forecast	+80.3%	A	20	53

Newsletter	1982 Gain (a)	Clarity Rating (b)	No. of Stocks in Portfolio 12/31/82	Holding Period (Days) (c)
MARKET AVERAGES				
DJIA	+19.6%			
NYSE Composite	+14.0%			
AMEX Market Value Index	+ 4.9%			
S&P 500	+14.8%			
NASDAQ OTC Composite	+18.7%			
Wilshire 5000	+12.9%			

Notes:
(a) Some letters precisely specify all elements to construct a model portfolio, thus rating an A. But many indicate allocations unsystematically and in general terms. Where such vagueness is acute—C or D—measuring the portfolio is necessarily more difficult.
(b) T-Bills don't count, so a portfolio entirely in T-Bills or the equivalent rates a "0".
(c) The average holding period of positions actually closed out by the portfolio during 1982, in days (unless the average period is longer than a year).
An "*" means that the figure is not available; an "N" means that no positions have been closed out; and an "?" means that the newsletter has been so low in clarity that a figure cannot be calculated with certainty.

PUBLICATIONS THAT SPECIALIZE IN LOW-PRICED STOCKS

A company named *Select Information Exhange*, 2095 Broadway, N.Y., N.Y. 10023, advertises frequently in *Barron's* and lists numerous publications, many dealing with low-priced stocks, that can be ordered through them. Some of the publications they list include the following:

The Cheap Investor: research reports on stocks under $10, new issues, and penny stocks.

Kon-lin Research and Analysis: market timing advice, specializes in listed low-priced stocks under $10. Analysis, buy and sell recommendations.

Penny Stock Journal: penny stocks and issues under $10 per share.

Astute Investor: identifies low-priced stocks with high earnings, growth, and net current assets.

National OTC Exchange: weekly newspaper concentrating on the national penny stock market, centered primarily in Denver.

Speculative Ventures: low-priced and OTC listed stocks with potential.

Bowser Report: newsletter features only stocks selling at $3 per share or less on NYSE, ASE, and OTC.

The Speculator: most active listed stocks under $20/ share.

The Penny Stock Newsletter: information on new companies in exceptional growth fields, many selling for $1 per share or less.

Samples of these and other publications may be ordered through *Select Information Exchange.* Examine the various ones to determine which ones you'll find more helpful. You may want to subscribe regularly to some of them. They provide additional sources of information, particularly on low-priced issues.

INDEX